PUBLISHED by PARABLES
Earthly Stories with a Heavenly Meaning

John Spiker,

GOD'S DIVINE UNDERSTANDING

A Handbook For Seeking God
While He is near and can be found
By
John Spiker

John Spiker,

John Spiker
Divine Understanding

Published By Parables
December, 2020

All Rights Reserved. No part of this book may be reproduced or utilized in any form or by any means, electronic or mechanical, including photocopying, recording, or by any information storage and retrieval system, without permission in writing from the author.

    ISBN 978-1-951497-88-0
    Printed in the United States of America

Readers should be aware that Internet Web sites offered as citations and/or sources for further information may have been changed or disappeared between the time this was written and the time it is read.

GOD'S DIVINE UNDERSTANDING

A Handbook For Seeking GOD
While He is near and can be found
By
John Spiker

John Spiker,

Introduction

At the time of this writing, there is a pandemic, the Coronavirus (COVID-19); that is causing the world to fall apart and crumble around us. The pace at which the coronavirus is spreading across the globe has led many to read the Bible in search of answers.

The fascination with the bible has grown more than ever in these times. Part of the fascination is due to the uncertainty of the coronavirus and our society's declining morals, rampant crime, and turmoil. People want answers.

Divine Understanding teaches us that everything revolves around GOD'S timing. The good, the bad, and the ugly, all revolve around GOD'S timing. It is because of the bad and ugly why I have written this book in these times. The purpose of this book ...to give faith, hope, and inspiration. To be a reminder of God's love, and to seek God while there is still time. A handbook that takes on the task of praying- A handbook that makes it easier to understand GOD, based on GOD'S Word. GOD'S Word will help make sense of everything going on around us these days.

Talk about GOD'S timing! I did not intend to write a book when everything is falling apart. But thanks to the pandemic of the Coronavirus, and GOD'S timing, that's exactly what I did.

Nothing motivates people like the bad and ugly of a pandemic to look for answers, hence GOD'S timing for this book. As it turns out, because of the coronavirus- this book may be just what you the reader needs. And at just the right time- GOD'S timing.

This book will not be an in-depth look at the end of the world. However, I did write chapter one on the end, because of everything that is now taking place. We must not ignore what the Scriptures say about the end-times. When we look at the end-times events through scripture, they become clear.

I encourage the reader to seek a better understanding of the end times. It is important that we be aware of the signs of the time. The reader should seek a better understanding of matters of their eternal significance.

At the time of this writing- there is no known cure or vaccine for the coronavirus. Many have taken these factors as evidence of the virus's supposed connections to biblical prophecy and end times.

It is my hope this book will give you the reader the answers you are searching for. Although the Bible was written thousands of years ago, it holds the answers for everything going on in our time.

As the Coronavirus is sweeping the globe and causing panic. Now would be a good time to shift your perspective...We have the chance to abstain from worldly things and seek GOD Almighty.

Because there is still time to seek the Lord; seek Him while you still can. Look for Divine Understanding. Take the time to learn some Valuable Lessons from the Bible and grow in your faith, plant some seeds of faith and seek GOD'S will. But most importantly Pray.

    My hope is this book will teach you to take the time to seek GOD'S Will and Divine Understanding for you. And how important it is to take the time to Prayer GOD'S Words back to Him. (See chapter 6).

John Spiker,

Chapter 1

Keys to Understanding Salvation, the Bible and the End Times.

Whether you are new to your Christian life or have been at it for some time. There are some words and phrases that we all need to know to understand our Salvation, the Bible, and the end times. These phrases will help us make sense of everything going on around us these days.

Therefore, I have made the point to go over some of the more critical words and phrases from the Bible that I use in this book. In no particular order here are some critical phrases to know and understand, we will go over these in later chapters.

1. *The first key phrase you should know about understanding GOD, and the end, is in understanding how Jesus Christ paid a ransom for us.* In 1Peter we see how Jesus paid that ransom, and we see the first key phrase in understanding end times in these last days.

[1Pe 1:18-20 NLT] *For you know that God paid a ransom to save you from the empty life you inherited from your ancestors. And the ransom he paid was not mere gold or silver. It was the precious blood of Christ, the sinless, spotless Lamb of God. God chose him as your ransom long before the world began, but he has now revealed him to you in these last days.*

The scriptures above tells us how Jesus Christ paid a ransom for our sins through His death. It explains how GOD revealed this to us in these last days: The phrase last days is a clue as to when the end times started: Understand the end times started the day that ransom was paid!

It also states that GOD chose Jesus before the world began. This is Divine Understanding! This is of the utmost importance to understand. As someone once said: Salvation is free, but not cheap...it did costs Jesus Christ, His life.

GOD loved His Creation, us humans so much that He gave His only son as a ransom so that everyone who has faith in Him will have eternal life and never die. Divine Understanding teaches us that GOD loves us and wants us to know Him so He can fill us with peace and give us Salvation. Jesus came so that everyone would have life and have it in its fullest.

The question that gets asked is since GOD planned for us to have peace and life, why are we so far from GOD? We became separated from GOD when Adam sinned. Since that time, the beginning of time, we have chosen to disobey GOD and go our own way. Understand by the beginning of time I mean from the time of man and the creation of the universe **[Rom 5:12 NLT] 12**

When Adam sinned, sin entered the world. Adam's sin brought death, so death spread to everyone, for everyone sinned. [Rom 3:23 CSB] 23

For all have sinned and fall short of the glory of God.

[Rom 5:12 CSB] 12 Therefore, just as sin entered the world through one man, and death through sin, in this way death spread to all people, because all sinned.

It is because of sin that we are so far from GOD. Adam's one sin brought death to everyone. From one man we all are condemned. From one man we are saved. Jesus Christ's one act of righteousness brings us Salvation. In that one act of righteousness, Jesus took away our sins. Understand there is no sin in Jesus Christ.

[Rom 5:18-19 NLT] 18 Yes, Adam's one sin brings condemnation for everyone, but Christ's one act of righteousness brings a right relationship with God and new life for everyone. Because one person disobeyed God, many became sinners. But because one other person obeyed God, many will be made righteous.

[1Jo 3:5 NLT] 5 And you know that Jesus came to take away our sins, and there is no sin in him.

There is only one way to reach GOD. Jesus Christ died for our sins; Jesus Christ is GOD'S Son. He is the only one who can bring us back to GOD. Jesus died on the Cross and rose from the grave. He paid the penalty for our sin and bridged the gap between GOD and people. Jesus Christ is the mediator of a better covenant established on a super promise, whoever believes in Him, will have eternal life.

[1Ti 2:5 CSB] 5 For there is one God and one mediator between God and humanity, the man Christ Jesus,
[Heb 8:6 CSB] 6 But Jesus has now obtained a superior ministry, and to that degree he is the mediator of a better covenant, which has been established on better promises.

2. *The second key phrase you should know about understanding GOD, and the end, is the term ages:*

The Bible talks about "ages" as periods of history over which GOD rules. An age means a time period. There are ages that pertain to the people of Israel. There are ages that pertain to the Gentiles. There are even ages that pertain to angels. There are ages that pertain to the Son of GOD.

The age we now live in is called: the age of grace, or the church age, the last times, and end of the age. No more ages are to come before Jesus Christ is to return, He will come in this age. Understand no one knows how long this age will last. Look at this again, no more ages to come...before Jesus Christ is to return. Make no mistake, He will come in this age.

But the Bible does speak of an age to come after this age. The Millennium Kingdom. This is the time Jesus sets up His Kingdom on earth for a thousand years.

3. *The third key phrase you should know about understanding GOD, and the end: is understanding the term Law and the Cursed Ones:*

Before Jesus, GOD made a covenant with Moses, in that covenant GOD gave the law. We now know that Jesus negotiated a better covenant then the law.

GOD gave the Law of Moses. The Law of Moses (also called Old Testament Law, Mosaic Law, or just The Law) regulated almost every aspect of Hebrew life. The Ten Commandments are just part of the law, called the morals law.

The truth no one could live by the Law, it was given so sin and trespass might increase to bring eternal life through Jesus Christ our Lord. We will go over the law in chapter 3 in detail.

Rom 5:20-21 NIV] The law was brought in so that the trespass might increase. But where sin increased, grace increased all the more, so that, just as sin reigned in death, so also grace might reign through righteousness to bring eternal life through Jesus Christ our Lord.

Understand, GOD gave the law where no one is able to keep it perfectly. The Law is the issue that must be dealt with in order to bring us into a right relationship with GOD. The Bible says all who try to live by the law are under a curse, because they must do everything written in the law. The curse is death.

[1Jo 3:4 NLT] 4 Everyone who sins is breaking God's law, for all sin is contrary to the law of God.

Cursed Ones: All who rely on the law are under a curse. Jesus Christ redeemed all from the curse of the law. The curse was death.

[Gal 3:10 NLT] 10 But those who depend on the law to make them right with GOD are under his curse, for the Scriptures say, "Cursed is everyone who does not observe and obey all the commands that are written in GOD's Book of the Law."

[Gal 3:13 KJV] 13 Christ hath redeemed us from the curse of the law, being made a curse for us: for it is written, Cursed [is] everyone that hangeth on a tree:

4. *The fourth key phrase you should know about understanding GOD, and the end: is understanding the term GOD'S Grace:*

Grace is a gift from GOD the Heavenly Father given through His Son, Jesus Christ. GOD does give out His Grace in many ways, and there are many kinds of grace, love, mercy, faith, peace, etc.

But the main Grace from GOD is in the form of Jesus Christ and eternal life. Everyone who believes in Him may not perish but may have eternal life. The Grace of Jesus Christ is our pardon for our sins. Christ paid that ransom, our sins are forgiven, and our relationship with GOD is restored.

[Rom 3:24-25 NIV] and all are justified freely by his grace through the redemption that came by Christ Jesus. GOD presented Christ as a sacrifice of atonement, through the shedding of his blood--to be received by faith..... He did this to demonstrate his righteousness, because in his forbearance he had left the sins committed beforehand unpunished--

GOD wants us to have the Grace that only Jesus Christ offers. , not because of anything we have done to earn it. We read in the Letter to the Ephesians: "For by grace you have been saved through faith, and this is not your own doing; it is the gift of GOD — not the result of works, so that no one may boast" (Ephesians 2:8-9). A gift that is always available, but one that can be refused.

[Jhn 1:16-17 ESV] For from his fullness we have all received, grace upon grace. For the law was given through Moses; grace and truth came through Jesus Christ.

5. *The fifth key phrase you should know about understanding GOD, and the end: is understanding the terms Last Days, Last Times, End Times, Last Times, Latter Days End of Time, and End of the Age:*

Basically, all talk about the end, and most often refers to the time of Tribulation. Understand the Bible uses such terminology in multiple ways. I will try and go over these terms but, care is needed as we look at the passages that use these terms. I will not go over these phrases in detail, it would take at least a chapter to go over all the terms.

All those listed above, have a future application. Therefore, when we read a passage in the Bible, which uses one of these phrases, we should recognize that the passages refer to the future, from the time of its writing.

They all mean an end will come. But they refer to an expression to a later period of time, and it is not always clear whether it means the end of the world. Certainly, the end of the world will come in the latter days, end times, last times, and end of the age.

These phrases basically describe the same period of time, events that will happen at the end of this age. Meaning the time of tribulation, the last seven years on earth before Jesus comes.

These events will result in the return of Jesus Christ and the establishment of the Kingdom of GOD here on earth. We read in Isaiah 2:2-4 about the time of the Millennium, where Jesus has established The Kingdom of GOD on this earth. It says: "it shall happen in the latter days". So, the phrase latter days could go into the Millennium.

[Isa 2:2 HNV] 2 It shall happen in the latter days, that the mountain of the LORD's house shall be established on the top of the mountains, And shall be raised above the hills; And all nations shall flow to it.

6. *The sixth key phrase you should know about understanding GOD, and the end: is understanding the terms Antichrists.*

The key is in understanding there is more than one that the Bible talks about. We also know we are in the last times because of all the Antichrists that have come and are coming.

Antichrist, Anti-messiah: Understand that scriptures teach us there are many antichrists and not just one. We mainly know of the antichrist from the book of revelation, a world ruler, who will come in the spirit of satan, the devil who will eventually come on the scene during the tribulation, just before the second coming of Jesus.

There will be a manifestation of the great and final antichrist, the antichrist who "is coming" in what we call the tribulation.

But anyone who does not confess that Jesus Christ is GOD and came in the flesh is an antichrist. The bible teaches us that we are living in the end times, the last hour, by seeing Anti-messiah, Antichrist.

The Bible verses below focus on warning against antichrists. These antichrists are not the same as the figure mentioned in the book of Revelation.

John begins with it is the last hour. He considered his time as part of the "last hour" or end times. It is clear the apostles believed he lived in some sense of "the end times," starting after the ascension of Jesus.

We understand the Apostle John did not mean the last hour, we understand this is used as a metaphor for the time of the end is near. This verse is a warning against antichrists, all antichrist from the time of Jesus till the end comes. John's reason for referring to the current time as "the last hour" was the emergence of so many of these antichrists he had personally encountered. Who was teaching against the true gospel of Jesus Christ.

[2Jo 1:7 NKJV] 7 For many deceivers have gone out into the world who do not confess Jesus Christ [as] coming in the flesh. This is a deceiver and an antichrist.

[1Jo 4:3 NKJV] 3 and every spirit that does not confess that Jesus Christ has come in the flesh is not of GOD. And this is the [spirit] of the

Antichrist, which you have heard was coming, and is now already in the world.

[1Jo 2:18 NKJV] 18 Little children, it is the last hour; and as you have heard that the Antichrist is coming, even now many antichrists have come, by which we know that it is the last hour.

[Gal 3:13 KJV] 13 Christ hath redeemed us from the curse of the law, being made a curse for us: for it is written, Cursed [is] everyone that hangeth on a tree:

7. *The seventh key phrase you should know about understanding GOD, and the end: is understanding the terms tribulation and Great Tribulation.*

The Bible tells us we will all ways have tribulation.

Jhn 16:33 NKJV] 33.......... In the world you will have tribulation; but be of good cheer, I have overcome the world."

But the tribulation we are concerned with is what we call the last seven years of tribulation. The last seven years before Jesus Christ comes. The tribulation we need to understand is the last seven years, it is at that time GOD will pour out His wrath upon the inhabitants of Earth. This terrible time of the Tribulation is coming, it will be far worse than any tribulation or biblical plagues we might have experienced as of yet, like the Coronavirus.

There are two parts to the Tribulation, three and a half years each. The Bible distinguishes between the two because the first three and a half years will only be the beginning of the horrors to come. The final three and half years is called The Great Tribulation:

We know that the seven-year tribulation period will begin when a peace agreement is reached between Israelis and its enemies. A ruler, believed to be the antichrist, the great and final antichrist, will be the one to make and break that treaty.

[Dan 9:27 NLT] 27 The ruler will make a treaty with the people for a period of one set of seven, but after half this time, he will put an end to the sacrifices and offerings.

Daniel speaks of The Great Tribulation in Daniel 7:25. He explains how it will last for three and half years. Jesus said in Matthew 24:15 that when you see the Abomination of Desolation, let those which be in Judaea flee because then shall there be great tribulation such as never has been before, nor ever again shall be. So, Jesus said the Abomination of Desolation is the event that will trigger the great tribulation.

[Mat 24:21-22 KJV] For then shall be great tribulation, such as was not since the beginning of the world to this time, no, nor ever shall be. And except those days should be shortened, there should no flesh be saved: but for the elect's sake those days shall be shortened.

We know from Daniel 9:27 that the Abomination of Desolation will occur halfway through the final seven-year period called Daniel's 70th week. We call this time the Tribulation.

[Dan 9:27 NIV] 27 He will confirm a covenant with many for one 'seven.' In the middle of the 'seven' he will put an end to sacrifice and offering. And at the temple he will set up an abomination that causes desolation, until the end that is decreed is poured out on him."

We understand that the Abomination of Desolation occurs in the middle of that seven-year period, and Jesus said that's the event that triggers the Great Tribulation. So, the first three and a half years of Daniel's 70th week will only be tribulation, it will not be a great tribulation at all, it doesn't start until the halfway point.

[Dan 7:25 NIV] 25 ………...The holy people will be delivered into his hands for a time, times and half a time.

Proof for a seven-year tribulation: The holy people will be delivered into his hands for a time, times, and half a time. We know that time as being one year, times is two years, and a half time is a ½ year. (1 year + two years + 1/2 years = 3.5 years).

Therefore, since we know that a peace treaty will trigger the seven-year Tribulation, understand the Abomination of Desolation is the event that will trigger the great tribulation.

Proof for the great tribulation: The following passages describe the length of the great tribulation. Forty-two months, one thousand two hundred and sixty days, all equals three and a half years.

[Rev 13:5 NKJV] 5 And he was given a mouth speaking great things and blasphemies, and he was given authority to continue for forty-two months.

[Rev 12:6 NKJV] 6 Then the woman fled into the wilderness, where she has a place prepared by GOD, that they should feed her there one thousand two hundred and sixty days.

What do we understand about the tribulation? We know that the overall tribulation will be for seven years. And we know that the seven years of tribulation will start with a peace treaty. And we know that the Abomination of Desolation is the event that will trigger the great tribulation. We know that Jesus Christ comes after those seven years of tribulation and sets up His Millennium Kingdom.

8. *The eighth key phrase you should know about understanding GOD, and the end: is understanding the term Rapture:*

A sudden vanishing of millions of Christians all around the world. Christians will vanish without a trace.

The Rapture-The Blessed hope: The word rapture is not in the Bible; we use the word to describe the phrase "caught up". The rapture is often referred to as the blessed hope. Because it provides assurance to believers who are concerned about the coming Tribulation and offers comfort to those who believe in GOD.

[1Th 4:17 KJV] 17 Then we which are alive [and] remain shall be caught up together with them in the clouds, to meet the Lord in the air: and so shall we ever be with the Lord.

[Tit 2:13 KJV] 13 Looking for that blessed hope, and the glorious appearing of the great GOD and our Saviour Jesus Christ;

The Rapture Is one of the most compelling and exciting events in the Bible. The Bible tells us the reason for this mass disappearance; the Church is not destined for the wrath of GOD. The Bible does warn believers to be ready and looking for the blessed hope. Therefore, we understand the Rapture is the blessed hope.

The rapture is a means of escape for the Church- all believers in GOD; living or who have died believing in the truth. Jesus Christ is the truth. I will not discuss the timing of the rapture; it would take a book all on its own. Understand it will come, either before the tribulation, during the tribulation, after the tribulation. It will come before Jesus Christ returns.

Christians are looking for the appearance of Jesus in the rapture, and not His return. Based on 1 Thessalonians 4:16-17. It is important to note this because this verse says, "to meet the Lord in the air." This means Jesus does not step foot on the earth at this time; believers will be called up to the clouds to meet Him. (Titus above says, glorious appearing). See below, it does not say return but the Lord Himself shall descend. He will be in the clouds and not return. Because when He does return, He will put foot on the Earth. In the rapture, Jesus will only appear in the clouds and not put foot on the earth. The second coming of Jesus is known as the "glorious appearing" and is described in detail in Revelation 19:11-20. And occurs at the end of the seven-year tribulation.

[1Th 4:16-17 KJV] For the Lord himself shall descend from heaven with a shout, with the voice of the archangel, and with the trump of GOD: and the dead in Christ shall rise first: Then we which are alive [and] remain shall be caught up together with them in the clouds, to meet the Lord in the air: and so shall we ever be with the Lord.

9. *The ninth key phrase you should know about understanding GOD, and the end: is understanding the term, Millennium Kingdom:*

This is the start of the thousand-year era of peace known as the Millennium. The Millennium is a time of peace and harmony on the earth when Jesus and the saints will rule in righteousness. The Millennium Kingdom will come after the seven years of tribulation. This is the time Jesus sets up His Kingdom on earth for a thousand years.

Although the word millennium never appears in the Bible, it speaks specifically and clearly of a period of 1,000 years that will serve as Jesus Christ Kingdom. During that time the world will finally achieve the elusive ideals of peace, prosperity, and purpose.

GOD'S chosen place that Jesus will rule from.... Jerusalem. Jerusalem will be a holy city and the center of the world for the Millennium Kingdom.

[Psa 132:13-14 NLT] For the LORD has chosen Jerusalem; he has desired it for his home. "This is my resting place forever," he

said. "I will live here, for this is the home I desired.

[Eze 43:7 NLT] 7 The LORD said to me, "Son of man, this is the place of my throne and the place where I will rest my feet. I will live here forever among the people of Israel..........

It is during the Millennium Kingdom that the devil will be locked in the bottomless pit for the thousand years of the Kingdom.

[Rev 20:1-3 NIV] And I saw an angel coming down out of heaven, having the key to the Abyss and holding in his hand a great chain. He seized the dragon, that ancient serpent, who is the devil, or Satan, and bound him for a thousand years. He threw him into the Abyss, and locked and sealed it over him, to keep him from deceiving the nations anymore until the thousand years were ended. After that, he must be set free for a short time.

10. *The tenth key phrase you should know about understanding GOD, and the end: is The Bible:*

Almost everyone has heard of the Bible. But most do understand it, or truly know what it is or where it comes from. GOD has revealed His mysterious plan for us through the Bible. The Bible is food for our souls, and it reveals GOD'S plan of salvation for us.

The Bible can be read as great literature, or as history. However, is the Bible fact or fiction? There are many questions over the Bible and a tone of controversy for those who do not understand it. The word Bible comes from the Greek word biblion, which means book. The Bible is the most remarkable book ever written. It is made up of 66 individual books. The Bible was written over 3 centuries, in three languages...... Hebrew, Aramaic, and Greek, and over approximately 1500 years by more than 40 authors, yet it remains unified from beginning to end. Point, when I say written, I do not mean translated from one language into another- but the language it was first written in.

But why so many different versions of the bible? Over time language has changed dramatically, Old English sounds and reads differently than modern English. So, to keep up with the changes in language, many new versions of the Bible have evolved. Because certain words have changed in meaning; With the new meaning the reader won't be confused while reading certain passages.

Once the manuscripts are determined for translation, the translators need to decide what translation philosophy they will follow. There are 3 main philosophies: The Bible has been translated into many languages from the biblical languages of Hebrew, Aramaic, and Greek into these philosophies.

I have to tell you; this is one part of my Bible study that is way out of my league. Major Bible translations typically reflect one of three general philosophies: formal equivalence, functional equivalence, and optimal equivalence.

The three philosophies meaning are:

Formal equivalence is a word-for-word translation and makes attempts to translate the

Bible as literally as possible, keeping the sentence structure and idioms intact if possible. This is a Literal translation. Attempts to keep the exact words and phrases of the original. It is faithful to the original text, but sometimes hard to understand. Also called Word-for Word focuses on translating word-for-word and strives to be as literal as possible. Examples: King James Version (KJV), New American Standard Bible (NASB).

Functional equivalence is typically referred to as a thought-for-thought translation. This is an attempt to translate the text, so it has the same effect on the current reader as it had on the ancient reader. Also called Dynamic equivalent. (thought for thought) translation. Attempts to keep a constant historical distance with regard to history and facts but updates the writing style and grammar. Examples: New International Version (NIV), Revised English Bible (REB).

Optimal equivalence falls between Formal equivalence and Functional equivalence, by balancing the tension between accuracy and ease of reading. While striving for precision in translation, it also seeks clarity to the modern-day reader. Christian Standard Bible (CSB). And the Holman Christian Standard Bible (HCSB).

There is one more that we should understand but is not a philosophy translates. It is a Free translation (paraphrase). Translates the ideas from the original text but without being constrained by the original words or language. Readable, but possibly not precise. Examples: The Living Bible (TLB), The Message.

1. Word-for Word: focuses on translating word-for-word and strives to be as literal as possible.

2. Thought-for-thought: focuses on a thought-for-thought (Dynamic equivalence) translation. Its goal is making the text easy to read and easier to understand.

3. Paraphrased: Paraphrased translations that use modern language and idioms to try to capture the thought and essence behind the original text., but paraphrase bibles make changes to the origin text.

The words, terms and translations, and versions are often used interchangeably. But we should look at these terms as separate. Translations have to do with language, and versions have to do with difference or variety, their philosophies.

My Personal Recommendation get more than one Bible. For your main reading and study. The most widely used Bible today in the U.S. is the New International Version (NIV). Or get (CSB) Christian Standard Bible, both are good choices. Then use them with others such as the New Living Translation (NLT) or word-for-word translation such as the English Standard Version (ESV). And the (NKJV). New King James Version is good if you use one of the others with it.

On top of all that, there are gender-neutral translations, where the term man comes in- it will use human or some other form that will be gender-neutral. These are translations that attempt to eliminate all male-only references in the Bible.

You can look at the Bible prefix to find out what type of Bible you have. But the best way is to go to the Bible website. Bibles change all the time, you could have a new version that changes to an all gender-neutral Bible, and not know it. Again, these are the ones that attempt to eliminate all male-only references in the Bible.

I firmly believe that the original manuscripts are the inspired Word of GOD, being the work of authors who were directed by the Spirit of GOD. But we know that some translations have made mistakes from one language to another.

[2Pe 1:20-21 NIV] Above all, you must understand that no prophecy of Scripture came about by the prophet's own interpretation of things. For prophecy never had its origin in the human will, but prophets, though human, spoke from God as they were carried along by the Holy Spirit.

To bring the feminist agenda to the Bible is wrong. I am talking only about the ones that change or try to eliminate every all male reference in the Bible. Some words previously translated as masculine do originally refer to both genders. In these cases, it is legitimate to change the reference. And at times makes more sense, the Bible versions that do this are ok, again it is only the ones that eliminate all male reference.

Compare, I believe it does make more sense to change.

[Rev 3:20 NIV] Here I am! I stand at the door and knock. If anyone hears my voice and opens the door, I will come in and eat with that person, and they with me.

Changed from: ***[Rev 3:20 NASB] 'Behold, I stand at the door and knock; if anyone hears My voice and opens the door, I will come in to him and will dine with him, and he with Me.***

Here is where I have the problem, "Son of man". VS "Son of human". Or "Child of Person". He to- person, someone, they. His to- your, their, those. Man to- mortals, human, person, those. Father to- parent. Son to- child. Brother to- fellow believer. Etc.

Can you see the problem? My point is stay away from Bibles that try to eliminate every male reference in the Bible. The Best thing you can do is compare different versions of the Bible you read; therefore, it is important to have more than one version of the Bible on hand.

A Brief Comparison of Major Bible Translations.
Word for Word Translation:

New American Standard, (NASB) Formal modern English; somewhat difficult but more readable than KJV. Gender-specific Bible versions.

Amplified, Modern English version from original Greek text. Has bracketed words and phrases to help explain more difficult and complicated passages. Some words previously translated as masculine do originally refer to both genders.

English Standard Version (ESV A literal translation that makes use of recently discovered sources. Easier reading than other word for word translations. Gender-specific Bible versions.

Original word	Modified by gender-neutral translations
he	person, someone, they
his	your, their, those
man (human race)	mortals, humans, humankind
man (male person)	anyone, person, those
men	those, people, others
father	parent
son	child
brother	fellow believer

King James Version (KJV) Difficult to read and understand due to 17th Century vocabulary and style. Uses no original or recently discovered sources. Gender-specific Bible versions.

New King James Version (NKJV) Taken directly from KJV but with more modern words. Choppy reading because it maintains 17th Century sentence structure. Gender-specific Bible versions.

Optimal equivalence Translation:

Christian Standard Bible (CSB). A translation philosophy that pursues both linguistic precision to the original languages and readability in contemporary English. Some words previously translated as masculine do originally refer to both genders.

Holman Christian Standard Bible (HCSB) Highly readable, accurate translation in modern English. Is a Good balance between word-for-word and thought-for-thought leans toward word-for-word.

Thought for Thought :

New Revised Standard Version (NRSV) still literal but moves in the thought-for-thought direction. Language not updated but tends to gender neutrality and political correctness.

New American Bible (NAB) Clear, straightforward translation from Greek language. The first Roman Catholic Bible in modern American English. New International Version (NIV) Completely new translation from oldest and best Hebrew, Greek, and Aramaic sources. Accurate, smooth reading version in modern English. Gender-neutral Bible versions.

New Living Translation (NLT)Converts of paraphrased Living Bible to a thought-for-thought translation. Highly readable in vocabulary and language. Gender neutral. Does not use original or recently discovered sources. Some words previously translated as masculine do originally refer to both genders.

Paraphrase Translation The Living Bible (TLB or LB) Paraphrase translation largely based on ASV of 1901. Modern language is very easy to read and understand. Also, a Catholic version.

The Message, Paraphrase translation by Eugene Peterson using 1980s American idioms. Easy to read but heavily criticized for scriptural deviations, altered meanings, informality, and lack of precision.

The Bible is a complex piece of work and can be hard to comprehend at times. The Bible is by far the most widely circulated book in the world. The Bible is divine in origin and all the Bible is GOD-Breathed! GOD revealed Himself in a variety of ways and used various methods to reveal the Scriptures to the chosen authors so they could record a permanent record concerning GOD.

[2Ti 3:16 NIV] 16 All Scripture is GOD-breathed and is useful for teaching, rebuking, correcting and training in righteousness,

What these authors wrote was GOD-Breathed. Every sentence, every word, every line is in complete agreement with the will of GOD. GOD used humans as authors to write down the words He wanted in the Bible and He watched over them as they did so.

Chapter 2
The End of the World.

Although, the end of the world is described in the Bible. First and foremost, no one knows the day or hour when the end will come. You might be surprised to learn what the Bible really says about the end of the world. Not only does the Bible give reasons to look forward to the end but it also acknowledges the frustration that can set in if the end seems to be overdue.

[Mat 24:36 NLT] "However, no one knows the day or hour when these things will happen, not even the angels in heaven or the Son himself. Only the Father knows.

There is no problem trying to understand the end. However, the issue lies when Christians begin to follow people who claim they know when the world will end, who have no true Biblical evidence.

GOD wants us to understand His plan for us, and the end of the world! The Scriptures in the Bible tells us so, that's why there are numerous end time events described in the Bible. These events are there to help us understand GOD and when the end could come.

Does the Coronavirus mean we are living in the end times, last days? The short answer is yes. Technically speaking the clock started ticking for the end, the last days- after a ransom was paid through the death and resurrection and ascension of Jesus Christ some two thousand years ago. The bible is clear, we have been living in the last days, the end times since Jesus paid that ransom. Make no mistake the end is near!

[1Pe 1:18-19 NLT] *For you know that God paid a ransom to save you from the empty life you inherited from your ancestors.*

We see in the scriptures below more proof we are living in the end times: 1John 2:18 where John says, "Little children, these are the end times." - 1Peter 4:7says;" The end of all things is near".

[1Jo 2:18 HNV] *Little children, these are the end times, and as you heard that the Anti-messiah is coming, even now many anti-messiahs have arisen. By this we know that it is the end times.*

[1Pe 4:7 NIV] *The end of all things is near. Therefore be alert and of sober mind so that you may pray.*

GOD reveals what He wants, and at the time He chooses to reveal what He wants. We know from scriptures that GOD has chosen to reveal to us that Jesus Christ paid a ransom in these last days. We know that GOD chose Him before the world began. We also know these are the end times. However, people say, the bible has been saying the end is near for over two thousand years.

How can one say the end to all things is near- if here we are some two thousand years later? It is all based on GOD'S timing! Understand, a day is like a thousand years to the Lord. Wherefore, if here we are two thousand years later for the Lord it has only been two days! GOD is not slow as we understand slowness.

[2Pe 3:8-9 NIV] But do not forget this one thing, dear friends: With the Lord a day is like a thousand years, and a thousand years are like a day. The Lord is not slow in keeping his promise, as some understand slowness. Instead he is patient with you, not wanting anyone to perish, but everyone to come to repentance.

[Psa 90:4 NLT] For you, a thousand years are as a passing day, as brief as a few night hours.

Wherefore, if we have been living in end times since Jesus Christ time... how can that be considered near?... Knowing that Jesus could come anytime. Hence the end is near. You see the truth is Jesus could come anytime in this age. So, He is near, but how near no one knows. But we will go over some signs to look for...like the Coronavirus.

For many people it does feel like the end of the world is near, as we live in these last times. However, the end basically hinges on the end of this age, and the return of Jesus Christ.

I know that I am repeating myself, but I want everyone to understand the end times are not the same as the last days, the tribulation. The end of the world comes in what we call the tribulation. The tribulation is the last days: which will be the last seven years on earth.

If the end times are here, then the end is near. Therefore, we understand the end is coming. We know there are no more ages to come, before Jesus returns, this is the last age...before He comes. But only GOD knows when Jesus will come.

One thing is for sure, our salvation is nearer now than anytime before. The Bible teaches us: Time to walk-up and understand the present times.

[Rom 13:11 NIV] And do this, understanding the present time: The hour has already come for you to wake up from your slumber, because our salvation is nearer now than when we first believed.

But when is the end, if we are living in the last times? Let us see what scriptures have to say about these times. No one knows the day or hour when the end will come. But there are end time events described in Scriptures to help us understand when the end will come.

Although, Christian predictions typically refer to events like the rapture, the Great Tribulation, the Last Judgment, and the Second Coming of Christ, as the end of time. Understand that the End of Days/ last days are the tribulation. The last seven years on earth. The bible teaches perilous times will come in these last days.

[2Ti 3:1 KJV] This know also, that in the last days perilous times shall come.

Jesus warned us about what the conditions would be like prior to His return. The bible is very clear about these conditions and events that will lead up to His second coming. The scripture below is talking about the time we now live in.

[2Ti 3:1-5 NKJV] But know this, that in the last days perilous times will come: For men will

be lovers of themselves, lovers of money, boasters, proud, blasphemers, disobedient to parents, unthankful, unholy, unloving, unforgiving, slanderers, without self-control, brutal, despisers of good, traitors, headstrong, haughty, lovers of pleasure rather than lovers of God, having a form of godliness but denying its power. And from such people turn away!

Perilous times show us that we are in the end times and we know that the clock for the end has been ticking for a long time now, over two thousand years. Indeed, with the coronavirus, and more and more unholy and unloving people, perilous times are here. We know that we have faced perilous times before and we know they will continue until the end of time.

Throughout Church history, people have faced perilous times, which have caused them to believe their generation was the one to see the end. Each generation throughout history believed they were in the last days. The truth is each of these generations has been living in the last times, but not the last days. Therefore, we know we have been in the last times for many generations now.

But the perilous times in the last days will be like nothing we have ever seen. It will be so bad that Jesus said, see I have told so ahead of time. And if that time was not shortened, not a single person would survive. So, by Jesus warning us ahead of time, He wanted us to understand the end times. Proof we are to understand the end times.

[Mat 24:25 NLT] *See, I have warned you about this ahead of time.*

[Mar 13:19-20 NLT] *For there will be greater anguish in those days than at any time since God created the world. And it will never be so great again. In fact, unless the Lord shortens that time of calamity, not a single person will survive. But for the sake of his chosen ones he has shortened those days.*

Because perilous times are here; whether it's a giant asteroid, a worldwide plague like the Coronavirus, or some other catastrophe. People are asking is this the end, the last seven years that the Bible talks about, called the tribulation. And where is GOD in all this?

The Bible is clear, the end is near, we are living in the end times. But no one can say when the end will come, only that it is near. Just know at any time the tribulation could start, or the rapture could come. Remember, if it took another two thousand years, that would only be two days for GOD.

Christians often ask three questions: Are we living in the End Times? Is the end of the world at hand? And, when is Jesus coming back? We will take a look and see what the Bible teaches us about these!

We know that the disciples of Jesus ask some of the same questions that we Christians ask today: The Olivet Discourse, is the name given to the teaching of Jesus Christ on the Mount of Olives. One of the main subjects is the end times. The Olivet Discourse is recorded in Matthew 24:1 – 25:46. Parallel passages are found in Mark 13:1-37 and Luke 21:5-36. The record in Matthew is the most extensive, so reference here will be to Matthew's Gospel.

The Olivet Discourse is Jesus' longest prophetic sermon and one of the most important passages in all the bible for end times. The disciples ask Jesus two questions, that had to do with the end. The first had to do with the destruction of the Temple, they asked; ("When will all this happen")? Which happened in A.D. 70.

The second question was a two-part question. ("What sign will signal your return, and the end of the world")? This is the one we will focus on.

[Mat 24:3, 25 NLT] Later, Jesus sat on the Mount of Olives. His disciples came to him privately and said, "Tell us, when will all this happen? What sign will signal your return and the end of the world?"

The signs that signal Jesus Christ return and the end of the world basically describe the same period of time, the tribulation period. But the signs that Jesus talked about are also the times we are in now, the end times. The end of this age will result in the return of Jesus Christ and the establishment of the Kingdom of God here on earth.

Jesus said there would be a period characterized by false Christs, wars, famines, earthquakes, persecutions, false religions, and more in the end. To better understand these events, I find it is easier to read them out of order, to know what time period the scripture is talking about. We will read Matthew 25,28, first. This is about the end times and tribulation period.

[Mat 24: 28 NLT] 25 See, I have warned you about this ahead of time. ... Just as the gathering of vultures shows there is a carcass nearby, so these signs indicate that the end is near.

Now we will read Matthew 4,5,6,7,8. This is about the end times, and the tribulation period.

4 Jesus told them, "Don't let anyone mislead you,...... 5 for many will come in my name, claiming, 'I am the Messiah.' They will deceive many. 6 And you will hear of wars and threats of wars, but don't panic. Yes, these things must take place, but the end won't follow immediately. 7 Nation will go to war against nation, and kingdom against kingdom. There will be famines and earthquakes in many parts of the world. 8 But all this is only the first of the birth pains, with more to come.

Now we will read Matthew 9,10,11,12. This is about the tribulation period.

9 "Then you will be arrested, persecuted, and killed. You will be hated all over the world because you are my followers. ...10 And many will turn away from me and betray and hate each other. 11 And many false prophets will appear and will deceive many people. 12 Sin will be rampant everywhere, and the love of many will grow cold. ...

Now we will read Matthew 22,24. This is about the tribulation period.

22 In fact, unless that time of calamity is shortened, not a single person will survive. But it will be shortened for the sake of God's chosen ones. ... 24 For false messiahs and false prophets will rise up and perform great signs and wonders so as to deceive, if possible, even God's chosen ones.

Now we will read Matthew 14,15,21. This is about the Great tribulation period.

14 And the Good News about the Kingdom will be preached throughout the whole world, so that all nations will hear it; and then the end will come. 15 "The day is coming when you will see what Daniel the prophet spoke about--the sacrilegious object that causes desecration standing in the Holy Place." (Reader, pay attention!) ... 21 For there will be greater anguish than at any time since the world began. And it will never be so great again.

Now that we understand the signs of the tribulation and the times, we live in. Back to the main question.... are we living in the last days, end times, last times, latter days, or the end of the age?

I usually respond with "Yes and No!" Such an answer requires an explanation. My explanation is that the Bible uses such terminology in multiple ways, (last days, end times, last times, latter days, end of the age).

The yes and no answer depends on how the question was asked, using the different terms above. All we must do is look at Isaiah 2:2-4 about the time of the Millennium. The time that Jesus has established The Kingdom of God on this earth.

Isaiah says: "it shall happen in the latter days". The phrase latter days here is talking about the Millennium and not the time of the tribulation. So, we see how latter days are not used just to describe the tribulation or end times.

[Isa 2:2 HNV] 2 It shall happen in the latter days, that the mountain of the LORD's house shall be established on the top of the mountains, And shall be raised above the hills; And all nations shall flow to it.

As we address the subject of the end, I have no desire to come across as a know-it-all. I give you my opinion of what the Bible has to say. But understand that I have prayed over and over for the answers. I encourage the reader to do the same.

Therefore, I say with the utmost confidence, the Coronavirus is not the end; just the beginning of what the Bible calls birth pains. When it comes to end-times, no one can be a hundred percent right. I also say the Coronavirus is not from GOD, but He will use it. I do believe that the coronavirus has come from the devil and that he is trying to use it to bring fear. I believe the devil is trying to move up GOD timeline. But GOD knows all and will used what the devil has done.

The bible uses a variety of descriptive terms to describe the end-times. But the term we are going to focus on... is birth pains. The upheaval we see in the world today is likened to the contractions experienced by a woman about to give birth, with those episodes increasing with frequency and intensity as time draws close to birth.

Just like it is with labor pains, where they become more frequent and more intense before the baby comes, but no one pain is the specific one for the baby to come. Therefore, just like labor pains progress in a woman in labor, we should expect the upheaval in the world to only increase.

We should expect wars, famines, earthquakes, and so on to become more and more frequent and intense before the end comes and the return of Jesus Christ – without any one of them being the specific sign of the end.

First and foremost, I do not think the coronavirus signals the end of days: Not- just- yet. Yes, the coronavirus is a plague for the last times, since we know that we have been living in them for many generations now.

However, it is of my opinion all that is going on now is what the Bible calls birth pains, which lead up to the last seven years. And as I have said, GOD did not create the coronavirus. It is all part of the devils plain to bring fear so he soon can take over. Know that GOD will use the Coronavirus for His Will, He did allow it to happen. The devil could not do it, if GOD did not allow it.

GOD has a plan for it. He may use it to bring many souls to Salvation, before He uses it to bring about an end. With the coronavirus, the devil satan thinks he is in control; but it is GOD who is in control. I believe before GOD allows the coronavirus to do the devils work...He will first use it to save souls. But I still believe it is a plague for the end times, but it did not come from GOD.

[Mar 13:8 HNV] 8 For nation will rise against nation, and kingdom against kingdom. There will be earthquakes in various places. There will be famines and troubles. These things are the beginning of birth pains.

Let me make something clear the future is unclear as to birth pains. No one knows how long these birth pains will last. Ironically, we know there is more to come.

I don't mean to make light of the pandemic or suggest that there aren't plenty of rational reasons to be concerned. Nevertheless, the Bible is clear: These diseases will worsen all the way up until the end. There may be a pause in the **upheaval**, in fact, there could be several pauses before the end comes. But the upheaval will **become more frequent and intense as time draws close to the end.**

So, we should expect diseases like the coronavirus to get worse, and to eventually spread like medieval pandemics and kill millions of people! God is already beginning to send a few globe-rattling events our way! The coronavirus and the other diseases breaking out today are only the beginning of birth pains.

We need to understand that we are now witnessing the fulfillment of numerous unique birth pains. These birth pains are setting the stage for the return of Jesus Christ. GOD has used birth pains to warn us throughout our history many of these warnings can be found in scriptures.

The Bible is our hope in understanding these birth pains. Moreover, we will need to have Faith in Jesus Christ in the days ahead, as we will see more and more of these birth pains. These birth pains will bring us closer to the time of tribulation. That time where GOD will pour out his wrath upon the inhabitants of the earth. The prophets of the Bible have predicted a precise pattern of events that will fit together during this period the end-of-days.

Even though the patterns of events we now see were predicted at different times long ago, they all properly fit the prophetic scenario- Jesus Christ will return. Every facet of prophecy in the Bible that is interpreted as occurring in the end-times relates to the return of Jesus Christ. These end time prophecies and their prophetic scenarios will not happen all at once, but over time just as they have been predicated over time.

But the two questions most people ask- are the prophecies that we now see happening, the ones found in the book of Revelation of the Bible, and are we in the last seven years?... The truth. Only time will tell. **Scriptures say, we will hear of wars and rumors of wars, but be not troubled; for such things MUST happen, but the end is not yet. If all this is birth pains, look for everything to get worse.**

[Mar 13:7 NKJV] 7 "But when you hear of wars and rumors of wars, do not be troubled; for [such things] must happen, but the end [is] not yet.

The book of Revelation is primarily about events that are to come and lead up to Jesus

Christ's second coming. The end-time culmination of the most devastating woes endured by mankind because of his rebellion against our Creator, GOD the Father.

Since the Book of Revelation contains the final chapters of the Bible and outlines what will happen in the last days, the last seven years. I will put my spin on what I believe is true and give you my opinion. It is true many religious-related end-time events are predicted to occur within this generation. And are often quoted from the book of Revelation. But should we be troubled by the book of Revelation?

NO. No, but we should understand the book of revelation. Especially when it talks about Tribulation. However, I do believe there is a time when we should be troubled... that time is the Great Tribulation found in the book Revelation.

We should think of the current outbreak of the Coronavirus as a preview of things to come, a little taste of what life will be like during the Tribulation. As we now know, the Tribulation is a relatively short period, it will last for only seven year. It's a time where everyone will experience worldwide hardships, disasters, famine, war and pandemics that will wipe out a lot of lives on the earth before the Second Coming takes place.

I am concerned, like a lot of people with our grocery stores being ransacked and of all the cancelations like schools, sports etc. And when I see people standing six feet apart from one another.

But I believe this is not the end of time. It all does feel apocalyptic, but is it the end, the last seven years, or just birth pains? I do not know; I cannot say for sure which it is!

Here is what I do know for sure: The Book of Revelation lays out a vision of the Last Times. If you see any of this Last Times happening, you know for sure you are in the Last Times, the last seven years. So what are they? We will take a brief look at 10 of those events. In no particular order:

1- An event we call the Rapture of the Church: A sudden vanishing of millions of Christians all around the world. Christians will vanish without a trace.

2- The Third Temple will be constructed in Jerusalem. The First Temple of Jerusalem, also known as Solomon's Temple, was destroyed. The second temple was rebuilt and destroyed by the Roman Empire, which started an exile of the Jewish people. The Bible says a Third Temple has to be re-build... when the Jewish people return from exile. The Jewish people have been returning to Jerusalem and are continuing today. So, it could be anytime now.

3- Peace Treaty- A ruler will make a peace treaty (covenant) with the nation of Israel for seven years. *[Dan 9:27 NLT] 27 The ruler will make a treaty with the people for a period of one set of seven, but after half this time, he will put an end to the sacrifices and offerings. And as a climax to all his terrible deeds, he will set up a sacrilegious object that causes desecration,* *until the fate decreed for this defiler is finally poured out on him."*

This ruler will not fully honor the covenant he made- but will break it in the middle of the 7 years. (In this passage one set of seven in those days implied seven years.) This is believed to be the start of the tribulation: The first three and half years of the tribulation. And the start of the Great Tribulation, after the covenant is broken; The final three and half years before Jesus Christ comes.

4- Two witnesses- Will be granted the power and authority to prophesy. *[Rev 11:3 NKJV] 3 "And I will give [power] to my two witnesses, and they will prophesy one thousand two hundred and sixty days, clothed in sackcloth."* Did you catch that, they will prophesy for three and half years? The first half of the tribulation.

5- Mark of the Beast-*[Rev 13:16-17 KJV] 16 And he causeth all, both small and great, rich and poor, free and bond, to receive a mark in their right hand, or in their foreheads: 17 And that no man might buy or sell, save he that had the mark, or the name of the beast, or the number of his name.*

6- Ezekiel's wars- take the time to read all of Ezekiel 38 and 39. Ezekiel talks about two wars, one has no name, this one we call the war with no name and the other is called Ezekiel's war. The one with no name, will result in Israel living in a time of peace. Which probably will involve nuclear weapons.

It is this war that may, and I repeat, may allow the Third Temple to be constructed in Jerusalem. Also, the Bible does not say who the war with no name is with.

Ezekiel's war comes after this war with no name. It will be an invasion of Israel from the North at the time when it will be living in peace: Which has never happened. Israel has never lived in a time of peace. But will after the war with no name happens.

Many Biblical Scholars believe this invasion, Ezekiel's war, will be led by Russia. And that Turkey, Syria, Libya, along with some others, will take part in that invasion. The Lord Himself will fight the battle for Israel.

God will display His awesome power and wrath in many ways: Some of which will be an earthquake, GOD will confound the enemies of Israel, so they fight against themselves and destroy each other. God will send great hailstones upon the enemy. GOD will use "fire and brimstone."

Israel will burn the weapons left on the battlefield for fuel, it will be enough to last them seven years. Therefore, Ezekiel's war could coincide with the tribulation, the last seven years. Or Ezekiel's war could commence near the beginning of the tribulation period, starting just before the tribulation starts.

7- A mighty shaking in the land of Israel- Also part of Ezekiel War- but deserves to have its own mention: **[Eze 38:19-20 NLT] 19 In my jealousy and blazing anger, I promise a mighty shaking in the land of Israel on that day. 20 All living things--the fish in the sea, the birds of the sky,** *the animals of the field, the small animals that scurry along the ground, and all the people on earth--will quake in terror at my presence. Mountains will be thrown down; cliffs will crumble; walls will fall to the earth.*

8- Scoffers-Scoffers will come in the last days. Mockers of the Word of GOD. And can mean one who mocks, ridicules, or scorns the belief of another. *[2Pe 3:3-4 NLT] 3 Most importantly, I want to remind you that in the last days scoffers will come, mocking the truth and following their own desires. 4 They will say, "What happened to the promise that Jesus is coming again? From before the times of our ancestors, everything has remained the same since the world was first created."*

[Jde 1:18 NLT] 18 They told you that in the last times there would be scoffers whose purpose in life is to satisfy their ungodly desires.

Know this, if I am right about the coronavirus pandemic being birth pains, it will make way for more ridicule and scoffers satisfying their ungodly desires.

Because more and more people are saying it is the end, and Jesus is coming, these scoffers will say where is the end, where is this Jesus. Not understanding more tribulation is to come before Jesus comes.

Yes, we have always had people mocking our faith and GOD, but we have not seen it on a level that the Bible talks about in the last days. I do believe the Coronavirus will amp up the ridicule.

While I believe the Coronavirus will end, the world will not be the same. It will open the door for the end to come. This virus will set the stage for the end. When this virus is over most people will forget how they turn to GOD for help.

Who cannot see that some great purpose and design is being worked out with the Coronavirus by GOD? I do believe that GOD is using the coronavirus, I believe GOD has a great purpose for the coronavirus. I see it as Winston Churchill saw WWII. Winston Churchill said how he understood GOD had a great purpose for WWII. And how GOD used it for His will. "He must indeed have a blind soul who cannot see that some great purpose and design is being worked out here below of which we have the honor to be the faithful servants." (Winston Churchill, to the United States Congress, WWII)

GOD is using the coronavirus for His will, if enough Christians pray... GOD will delay His judgments. This does not mean the coronavirus will not set the stage for the end to come, only everything I am saying will be delayed. It is an opportunity for Christians to pray, there is a pattern in the Bible where GOD'S judgments were delayed because of prayer but know at some point they will come.

The coronavirus may just be birth pains, but it will set the stage for everything to be able to happen in the tribulation. How long, it could be a short time before we see any results. However, it may take some time, a few years. But the ridicule, and scoffers will come right after the pandemic ends. Understand this, the coronavirus will be a springboard into the tribulation, I can't say when or how long it will take to happen.

9- The falling Away: Has more than one interpretation. The falling away is also used as an Apostasy. Which is a rejection of Christianity by someone who formerly believed as a Christian. Apostasy refers to: departure, revolt or rebellion. Therefore, this verse has more than one explanation or interpretation. ***[2Th 2:3 KJV] 3 Let no man deceive you by any means: for [that day shall not come], except there come a falling away first, and that man of sin be revealed, the son of perdition;***

Falling Away- The downward spiral of our global society, a departing of our morals and ethics. A falling away from the faith an Apostasy. It seems to be describing a spiritual collapse (Apostasy) and a departure. Departure here refers to the rapture of the church.

And at this time, we see the man of sin will be revealed. The man of sin is a person energized by Satan. This man will deceive many and is known by a variety of names- man of sin, the beast, the man of lawlessness and the Antichrist.

This antichrist, man of sin could be the one in the same, as the ruler who makes a peace treaty with Israel for seven years. Because this falling away could coincide with the Peace Treaty-signing, that will start the tribulation. And we know the peace will not come until the events in Ezekiel 38 and 39- come to pass.

10- Abomination of desolation. The Antichrist will cause the temple to become useless and empty. ***[Dan 11:31 NASB] 31 "Forces from him will arise, desecrate the sanctuary fortress, and do away with the regular sacrifice. And they will set up the abomination of desolation.***

The Third Temple will have been constructed in Jerusalem for this to happen. The Antichrist will do away with the regular sacrifice and make desolate the Third Temple; cannot be used for regular sacrifice anymore. The Temple will become unholy and will no longer be a righteous and holy temple. The abomination of desolation will trigger the Great Tribulation, the last three and a half years on earth.

By setting himself up as god, this will cause the temple to be *desolate:* ***[2Th 2:4 KJV] 4 Who opposeth and exalteth himself above all that is called God, or that is worshipped; so that he as God sitteth in the temple of God, shewing himself that he is God.*** This is where the antichrist sets himself as god in the temple. By setting himself up as god, causes the Abomination of desecrate.

A closer look at 2Thessalonians 2:1-4; as to the end of days. And the coming of our Lord Jesus Christ and our gathered to him. As with many scriptures there is more than one meaning, explanation, interpretation for the phrases that are used.

[2Th 2:1-4 NIV] Concerning the coming of our Lord Jesus Christ and our being gathered to him, we ask you, brothers and sisters, not to become easily unsettled or alarmed by the teaching allegedly from us--whether by a prophecy or by word of mouth or by letter-- asserting that the day of the Lord has already come. Don't let anyone deceive you in any way, for that day will not come until the rebellion occurs and the man of lawlessness is revealed, the man doomed to destruction. He will oppose and will exalt himself over everything that is called God or is worshiped, so that he sets himself up in God's temple, proclaiming himself to be God.

What phrases do biblical scholars understand through cross-referencing and study of the above scripture are important enough to take a second look at? Let us look at six of this:

1-Concerning the coming of our Lord Jesus Christ: and our being gathered to him: Relates to the time Jesus Christ comes for His church when it will be gathered to Him, meaning the rapture. The Rapture, when Jesus Christ comes to the clouds above the earth and catches up or raptures all Christians to meet Him in the air. Notice I did not say Jesus returns, but only comes to the clouds.

2- The Day of the Lord: Most biblical scholars associate the day of the Lord with two times periods. "The Day of the Lord" and "The Day." These days will occur when God's will and purpose for the world will be fulfilled. One key to understanding these phrases is to note that they always identify a span of time during which God personally intervenes in history, directly or indirectly, to accomplish some specific aspect of His plan.

The Day of the Lord usually identifies events that take place at the end of history the last seven years of tribulation. The Day, when used alone like this- always is associated with the Second Coming of Christ, when He returns. And is related to the setting up of His Millennium Kingdom.

3- Until *the rebellion occurs:* This is the falling away and Apostasy.

4- The *man of lawlessness is revealed:* This is the antichrist, the man of sin.

5- T*he man doomed to destruction:* Is the antichrist who is doomed, when Jesus Christ comes, He will do away with him.

6- *he sets himself up in God's temple, proclaiming himself to be God:* This is the Abomination of desecrate, by setting himself up as god, this will cause the temple to be *desolate.*

To summarize, according to *2Thessalonians 2:1-4; The* end cannot come until:

- "We are told don't let anyone deceive you in any way, for that day will not come until." The man of lawlessness is revealed, the man who is doomed to destruction, the antichrist. He is revealed by the one who makes the seven-year covenant with Israel.

- A peace treaty, covenant must be made with the nation of Israel for seven years, and then it must be broken after three and half years.

- The rapture must come.

- The rebellion must occur: This is the falling away and Apostasy.
- The Abomination of Desecration must happen.

Now add in the other events that are to happen before the end comes:
- A Third Temple will be constructed in Jerusalem.
- Two Witnesses will prophesy for three and half years.
- The mark of the beast must come.
- Ezekiel's wars, one with no name-will result in Israel living in a time of peace. Ezekiel's war invasion of Israel from the North must come.
- A mighty shaking in Israel.
- Scoffers, Mockers must come.

As we see GOD has told us how the world will end. The end of the world is a terrifying prospect. However, for Christians with Divine Understanding, the end of the world is anything but dreadful. The truth is....it is something we should actually look forward to.

[[2Ti 3:1 CSB] 1 But know this: Hard times will come in the last days.

I said this before but understand the coronavirus will be a springboard to the tribulation. Understand this could take some time but know that GOD is not slow. The tribulation will come and just at the right time. These scoffers will come to, as more and more people will be saying during and after the coronavirus, it is the end, and Jesus is coming.

Then these same scoffers will say where is the end, where is this Jesus. But understand, it might take two and three more events like the coronavirus or some other catastrophe to come before we see the full strength of these scoffers who mock the Lord's second coming.

But they will come, mockers who seek to convince others that the promise of our Lord's second coming is false based upon the passage of much time. These mockers could say something like...there is no visible evidence that Jesus will come. After all the coronavirus is gone, where is this tribulation you talk about?

I bet these scoffers will say something like the coronavirus is over, where is this Jesus, I thought YOU said he was coming. These people will mockingly ask, where is the promise of his coming? When all along it was, they who were saying it. Christians know scoffers will come, and they know Jesus will come again, but we also know to wait on GOD.

The truth is people don't handle delays very well, we simply do not like to wait. From their questions about the coming of our Lord's kingdom, it was evident the disciples were not excited about waiting either, most of them thought Jesus will come back in their lifetime.

We humans do not want to wait on anything, including GOD. But GOD'S promises never come too late; in truth, they are never late at all. However, the truth is we have been waiting on God all through history. Noah waited over 100 years or so for the flood to come upon the earth. Abraham and Sarah waited 25 years for the promise for a son. Abraham did not even possess the promised land in his lifetime, it was more than 400 years later that is his descendants took possession of the promised land.

After this coronavirus is over, mockers will believe they have given GOD plenty of time to fulfill His promise to return and will conclude that His time is up. Can you imagine them saying, If He hasn't come by now, He simply isn't coming.

2Peter 3 says it all, in his letter, Peter exposes these scoffers, mockers, along with their denials, following their own desires:

[2Pe 3:3-15 NLT] Most importantly, I want to remind you that in the last days scoffers will come, mocking the truth and following their own desires. They will say, "What happened to the promise that Jesus is coming again? From before the times of our ancestors, everything has remained the same since the world was first created." They deliberately forget that God made the heavens by the word of his command, and he brought the earth out from the water and surrounded it with water. Then he used the water to destroy the ancient world with a mighty flood. And by the same word, the present heavens and earth have been stored up for fire. They are being kept for the day of judgment, when ungodly people will be destroyed. But you must not forget this one thing, dear friends: A day is like a thousand years to the Lord, and a thousand years is like a day. The Lord isn't really being slow about his promise, as some people think. No, he

is being patient for your sake. He does not want anyone to be destroyed, but wants everyone to repent. But the day of the Lord will come as unexpectedly as a thief. Then the heavens will pass away with a terrible noise, and the very elements themselves will disappear in fire, and the earth and everything on it will be found to deserve judgment. Since everything around us is going to be destroyed like this, what holy and godly lives you should live, looking forward to the day of God and hurrying it along. On that day, he will set the heavens on fire, and the elements will melt away in the flames. But we are looking forward to the new heavens and new earth he has promised, a world filled with God's righteousness. And so, dear friends, while you are waiting for these things to happen, make every effort to be found living peaceful lives that are pure and blameless in his sight. And remember, our Lord's patience gives people time to be saved. This is what our beloved brother Paul also wrote to you with the wisdom God gave him--

The coronavirus will be the beginning of the falling Away- where some Christians will stop believing because Jesus did not come during the coronavirus. They most likely will be the ones whose faith was because of the pandemic. Or because Jesus coming is taking too long for them and will lose faith.

But understand GOD will use the coronavirus first for His Will to save souls! This could take some time, but when GOD is done using it for His good- it will be used by the devil satan to bring more fear, and scoffers.

One last look at what the bible says about the last days:

[2Ti 3:1-5 CSB] But know this: Hard times will come in the last days. For people will be lovers of self, lovers of money, boastful, proud, demeaning, disobedient to parents, ungrateful, unholy, unloving, irreconcilable, slanderers, without self-control, brutal, without love for what is good, traitors, reckless, conceited, lovers of pleasure rather than lovers of God, holding to the form of godliness but denying its power. Avoid these people.

I do not like to prophesy, but If GOD does delay His judgments. I believe it will be no more than 10 years, for reasons I will not go into. So, understand what I am saying.... there could be a 10-year delay in birth pains. And if there is a delay, there will be a great awakening in these last days. Because GOD is not finished with us yet. And I am not saying that will not experience those birth pains to some degree during this great awakening.

But GOD will use this time as an opportunity to release His power and love. During this delay GOD will still chastise us, but to a smaller degree.

I do believe in the imminent second coming of Jesus Christ. I am not saying GOD will come in 10 years. Only if there is a delay from this **Coronavirus, it will be no more than 10 years. I do believe Jesus will come so. I will not say when, but His imminent return is fast approaching.**

Please do not try and set a date from what I am saying...only GOD knows the date and time of His judgments. It is only that I believe the evil of mankind will increase, because the devil is loose, and GOD will have had enough. All that I am writing about could come anytime, it also could take another thousand years. But because the coronavirus is here, I say evil and wickedness will increase because the virus is a sign of the times.

But here is what I believe will come next on our timeline, within 10 years. Look for a great awakening, and scoffers to come, Ezekiel's wars: The one with no name will come first and will result in Israel living in a time of peace. Sometime after the war with no name, Ezekiel's war, the invasion of Israel from the North will come. Then the Peace Treaty will be signed to start the tribulation. The Peace Treaty could come before Ezekiel's war but after the war with no name.

The tribulation will come after these two wars or coincide with Ezekiel's war. Again, Ezekiel's war occurs near the beginning of the final seven-year tribulation period and after the war with no name. Ezekiel's war will bring about much devastation to the planet. And will only intensify until the second coming of Christ. While Israel's victory in this war will encourage Israel, the world will be severely traumatized by this war. And we know that The Lord Himself will fight the battle for Israel.

This point cannot be overstated, because Ezekiel's war and the events following it will instill such fear and insecurity in humanity as to pave the way for the coming of an "antichrist." And the coming of the two witnesses.

The world seems more fractured and falling apart more and more each day. Will the world ever be the same again? The answers can be found in the Bible! If we believe that Jesus could come back any time, then we should not be sitting back, but be looking for Him.

So will the events of the end of this age, and the return of Jesus Christ in the new age strike you with hope and joy, or dread. As for me and my family, we will live with hope. Because of GOD'S mercy and glory, we have a living hope through the resurrection of Jesus Christ from the dead.

[1Pe 1:3 CSB] Blessed be the God and Father of our Lord Jesus Christ. Because of his great mercy he has given us new birth into a living hope through the resurrection of Jesus Christ from the dead.

[Jhn 3:16-18 NET] For this is the way God loved the world: He gave his one and only Son, so that everyone who believes in him will not perish but have eternal life. For God did not send his Son into the world to condemn the world, but that the world should be saved through him. The one who believes in him is not condemned. The one who does not believe has been condemned already, because he has not believed in the name of the one and only Son of God.

Chapter 3
Seek GOD while He is near. Find faith while there is still time.

[Hos 10:12 KJV] .... for [it is] time to seek the LORD, till he come and rain righteousness upon you. This Scripture teaches: for it is time to seek the Lord. Seek the Lord, till He comes and rains righteousness upon you. Know this, He will come at the end of this age.

We see in Joel 2:12 where the Lord says, "Turn to me now, while there is time. Give me your hearts. Come with fasting, weeping, and mourning. *[Joe 2:12 NLT] That is why the LORD says, "Turn to me now, while there is time. Give me your hearts. Come with fasting, weeping, and mourning.*

According to the Bible, we are now living in The Age of Grace, sometimes called "The Church Age." But this age won't last forever. Because someday the period of grace will suddenly be over, and it will be time for judgment. For GOD has set a day for judgment.

[Act 17:31 NIV] 31 For he has set a day when he will judge the world with justice by the man he has appointed. He has given proof of this to everyone by raising him from the dead."

[Isa 55:6-11 NKJV] 6 Seek the LORD while He may be found, Call upon Him while He is near.

The above would imply that there may be a time when GOD cannot be found. Yes, the Bible does imply at some point in time GOD will withdraw His Spirit from us. ***[Gen 6:3 HNV] 3 The LORD said, "My Spirit will not strive with man forever,***

[Psa 32:6 NIV] 6 Therefore let all the faithful pray to you while you may be found;...

As you can see GOD's Spirit will not be with man forever. The Bible teaches us to seek GOD while He can be found, and to pray to Him while He is Near. The time is now, the age we now live in.

The Age of Grace-will be coming to an end. It is GOD's wish that each and every Christian seek to establish a close, intimate, personal relationship with the Lord. This relationship is of extreme importance that every person enters into a personal relationship with the Lord, so that He can then extend His perfect plan and destiny for their lives.

What is really important in this life? I bet with the coronavirus; some people have changed their minds! The Bible tells us what the big picture should be...where our priorities should be. Which is to set our priorities on our Salvation by seeking GOD.

[Psa 10:4 NLT] The wicked are too proud to seek GOD. They seem to think that GOD is dead.

[Psa 69:32 NLT] The humble will see their GOD at work and be glad. Let all who seek GOD's help be encouraged.

[Mat 6:33 NLT] Seek the Kingdom of GOD above all else, and live righteously, and he will give you everything you need.

[Act 17:27 NLT] "His purpose was for the nations to seek after GOD and perhaps feel their way toward him and find him--though he is not far from any one of us.

The Bible talks about a Day of Judgment, many believe it will be too late on that day to seek GOD. This day of judgment that the Bible talks about is the time when the Son of Man comes, who is Jesus Christ, who GOD raised from the dead. The day of judgment is that time that GOD will withdraw His Spirit. His Spirit will no longer be found by the cursed ones, wicked people who refuse to believe in Jesus Christ. These people are the ones who try to live under the law. And not GOD grace.

[Mat 25:31-34, 41 NLT] "But when the Son of Man comes in his glory, and all the angels with him, then he will sit upon his glorious throne. All the nations will be gathered in his presence, and he will separate the people as a shepherd separates the sheep from the goats. He will place the sheep at his right hand and the goats at his left. "Then the King will say to those on his right, 'Come, you who are blessed by my Father, inherit the Kingdom prepared for you from the creation of the world. ... "Then the King will turn to those on the left and say, 'Away

with you, you cursed ones, into the eternal fire prepared for the devil and his demons.

To summarize, we are living in an age where GOD still grants grace to those seeking salvation through His son Jesus Christ. The age of grace is the time in which Jesus Christ died for the sins of the sinner, paid that ransom. It is because of that ransom that we all can all have forgiveness for our sins.

Understand GOD has extended His mercy and grace to whoever will receive it. GOD's offer of forgiveness still stands for now. But this period of grace will not go on indefinitely and someday it will be too late for men and women to repent and turn to the Lord Jesus Christ for Salvation.

The age of grace, also called "the Church Age," began on the Day of Pentecost. And as we now understand was made possible by Jesus Christ's sacrificial death on the cross for all sin: Through His death and resurrection.

The Day of Pentecost is one of the most significant events recorded in the Bible; it is the day the Holy Spirit came down to permanently indwell believers, and when the church age began. Pentecost is regarded as the birthday of the Christian church. Pentecost is the festival when Christians celebrate the gift of the Holy Spirit.

The Christian holy day of Pentecost, which is celebrated fifty days after Easter Sunday. Commemorates the descent of the Holy Spirit upon the Apostles and other followers of Jesus Christ while they were in Jerusalem. They were there celebrating the Feast of Weeks, also called. Shavuot, a Jewish harvest festival.

The harvest festival of Shavuot has a double significance. It marked the all-important wheat harvest in the Land of Israel. And it commemorates the anniversary of the day when GOD gave the Torah to the nation of Israel assembled at Mount Sinai. (The Torah, are the first five books of the Old Testament of the Bible.)

Moses, ascended to the top of Mount Sinai to meet with GOD who gave him the Ten Commandments, a moral code and the Law (The Torah). We know that the Ten Commandments were inscribed on two tablets of stone.

[Exo 34:22 NIV] 22 "Celebrate the Festival of Weeks with the firstfruits of the wheat harvest,

At Pentecost, the apostles were celebrating this festival when the Holy Spirit descended on them. It sounded like a very strong wind, and it looked like tongues of fire. The apostles then found themselves speaking in foreign languages, inspired by the Holy Spirit.

How long will the Age of Grace last? Only GOD knows. But know this - time is short. And know this- many Bible Scholars believe that when Jesus Christ returns...anyone who has rejected Him; there will not be no more chances. They will be judged for their sins.

What about the Rapture? Is the Rapture not a time GOD will withdraw His Holy Spirit? The Rapture- an end-time event: That Christians believe they will rise in the clouds, to meet the Lord in the air before He establishes His kingdom on earth. It is the time Jesus will come for His Church; an event commonly referred to as the "Rapture."

It is important to note that the Rapture will bring the end of the Church age. Some believe that it will be too late to seek GOD then, time has run out. Because the Holy Spirit is no longer with us.

Also, it is believed that if one dies without receiving Jesus Christ as Lord and Savior...it will be too late for them to repent and receive Salvation, because they have rejected Salvation. That's because if we die without receiving Christ as Savior— we have rejected Him—there aren't any more chances for someone who has rejected Jesus Christ. That person will be judged for their sins.

I cannot write this chapter without saying.... I never take the position that GOD is finished with someone. Only GOD knows if He is finished with someone or not. Wherefore, I take the position that the last chance will be at Judgment. I believe GOD in all His Mercy, will give one last chance to receive Jesus Christ. But, after that, make no mistake there will be no more chances.

So, if one dies without Jesus Christ, or the Rapture has come; they may have a last chance: I repeat; may have a chance at the time of judgement. But only GOD knows. Therefore, we should seek GOD now! While He is near. Call on the Lord Jesus Christ while you still can and be saved from your sins and receive your Salvation.

Christians believe in the second coming of Jesus Christ. His return from heaven will be personal, visible and glorious, a blessed hope for which we should constantly watch and pray.

This expectation of Jesus Christ coming should be a motivation for holy living, as well as a source of comfort and for seeking GOD. GOD has assured us that the end of the age will mark the beginning of a new age, one with GOD. But no man knows the day or the hour when this will take place.

Understand GOD is not slow in His coming. He is waiting with open arms for all of us to approach Him. Waiting for an intimate relationship, intimate fellowship, intimate prayer and dialogue. GOD says we can have conversations about anything and everything, that is how it becomes a personal relationship.

Bottom line: Seek GOD now, do not be afraid to establish a one-on-one relationship with Him. The key to establish this relationship is you have to be willing to seek the Lord. Seek the Lord while there is still time. Find faith in Him while there's still time. **The way the Lord works is fascinating. However, what is most fascinating is how GOD works in our lives through our faith.**

The Bible tells us that we have to be the ones to first initiate some kind of contact with GOD to find faith. We have to be the ones to start out actual seeking and drawing near to GOD. Seek, and then you will find GOD. Draw near to GOD, and then He will draw near to you. Ask, and then you will receive. Knock, and then the doors will open up for you.

[Luk 11:9-10 NIV] "So I say to you: Ask and it will be given to you; seek and you will find; knock and the door will be opened to you.

For everyone who asks receives; the one who seeks finds; and to the one who knocks, the door will be opened.

The Bible tells us to seek GOD with all our heart, and all our soul. And to pour out our hearts to Him. Rome was not built overnight, and neither will your personal relationship with GOD come overnight. It will take time to develop spiritual discernment.

[Ch 28:9 CSB] "As for you, Solomon my son, know the GOD of your father, and serve him wholeheartedly and with a willing mind, for the LORD searches every heart and understands the intention of every thought. If you seek him, he will be found by you, but if you abandon him, he will reject you forever.

All GOD asks of us is that we give Him the best effort we can in our spiritual development. If we do this, know that GOD will meet us halfway So you will not have to do it all on your own.

[Psa 62:8 NIV] Trust in him at all times, you people; pour out your hearts to him, for GOD is our refuge.

[Mar 12:30 NIV] Love the Lord your GOD with all your heart and with all your soul and with all your mind and with all your strength.'

Understand that we are not dealing with only one GOD – but one GOD in three separate and complete Persons. – GOD the Father, His Son Jesus Christ, and the Holy Spirit. All Three of Them want to have a personal relationship with us.

The Bible tells us that GOD shows no personal favoritism to any person He has ever created. What this means is that we are all equal in the eyes of GOD.

[Act 10:34 NLT] Then Peter replied, "I see very clearly that GOD shows no favoritism.

[Rom 2:11 NLT] For GOD does not show favoritism.

[Jas 3:17 NLT] But the wisdom from above is first of all pure. It is also peace loving, gentle at all times, and willing to yield to others. It is full of mercy and good deeds. It shows no favoritism and is always sincere.

GOD the Father, Son, and Holy Spirit have an equal and unconditional love for each person He has ever created. They give everybody the same attention, to those who seek them. What this means is that you can establish and develop just as much of a personal relationship with GOD, the Son and Holy Spirit as everybody else.

Everyone needs to think about this...the one and only GOD of this entire universe wants to be your best Friend. A true best Friend who will never harm you, hurt you, mistreat you, lie to you, leave you, or forsake you! All you have to do is seek Him. Seek GOD while you still can.

[Isa 55:6-11 NKJV] Seek the LORD while He may be found, Call upon Him while He is near.

[Psa 32:6 NIV] Therefore let all the faithful pray to you while you may be found;

Therefore, let all the faithful pray to you while you may be found"! Pay to GOD while He can be found, pray to have that personal relationship with Him. Start out actually seeking GOD, remember you must start the conversation. Draw near to GOD, and then He will draw near to you. Remember this...you can lead a horse to water, but you cannot make it drink the water. Drink from the fountain of living waters.

[Isa 12:3 NIV] With joy you will draw water from the wells of salvation.

[Jhn 4:10 NLT] Jesus replied, "If you only knew the gift GOD has for you and who you are speaking to, you would ask me, and I would give you living water."

Jesus told us that He Himself is the fountain of living waters and that we will never hunger or thirst again if we would only be willing to drink directly from Him.

[Jhn 7:38-39 NLT] Anyone who believes in me may come and drink! For the Scriptures declare, 'Rivers of living water will flow from his heart.' (When he said "living water," he was speaking of the Spirit, who would be given to everyone believing in him. But the Spirit had not yet been given, because Jesus had not yet entered into his glory.)

GOD has offered us much more than mere water. He has offered us the blood and body of Jesus Christ. But like that horse, you decide whether to drink of it or not. GOD has already shown us how much He loves all of us by being willing to sacrifice His one and only Son.

All GOD is asking from each one of us is that we be willing to fully trust Him, and then be willing to enter into an intimate, personal relationship with Him. We now understand, GOD is not slow in His coming as some would say. He is waiting, waiting for every person He has created to come to Him and establish a close, intimate, personal relationship with Him. GOD is patiently waiting so everyone can be saved.

[2Pe 3:15 NLT] And remember, our Lord's patience gives people time to be saved. This is what our beloved brother Paul also wrote to you with the wisdom GOD gave him--

If you will just seek after GOD. Seek after Him with all of your heart, with all of your mind, and with all of your soul. You will have a personal relationship with Him, thereby you will be saved from the curse of death.

[Psa 14:2 NIV] The LORD looks down from heaven on all mankind to see if there are any who understand, any who seek GOD.

Psalm above says GOD is actually looking down from heaven. To see if any will seek Him. Think about this for just one moment.... The one and only all-powerful GOD is actually looking to see if any will seek Him. He is looking down from His throne in Heaven to see if any will seek after Him.

It is pretty amazing to think that GOD has an open invitation for all of us to seek Him. It is wonderful to know that if we attempt to seek after Him, we will actually find Him. Scriptures tell us, He is not far from any one of us. The Bible tells us- that if we make an attempt to seek GOD, we will be able to find Him, after all, He is not far from us at any time.

Remember you must start that conversation, then GOD will be able to communicate back to you. He is willing to meet us halfway! How incredible and awesome that is to know. GOD can be found, but only if we are willing to make enough of an effort on our end to seek directly after Him, seek Him with all our heart.

[Jer 29:13 NIV] You will seek me and find me when you seek me with all your heart.

My hope is that the message from the Bible is coming through loud and clear. GOD is seeking those who are willing to seek after Him with all their heart and soul. Understand GOD will not settle for anything less. It is just as important to know that if you forsake GOD, He will do the same to you!

We must get to know the GOD of our ancestors intimately. We must worship and serve Him with our whole heart and a willing mind. GOD knows every heart, and He knows our thoughts. Do not abandon Him, seek Him with all your heart.

[1Ch 28:9 NLT] "And Solomon, my son, learn to know the GOD of your ancestors intimately. Worship and serve him with your whole heart and a willing mind. For the LORD sees every heart and knows every plan and thought. If you seek him, you will find him. But if you forsake him, he will reject you forever.

GOD rewards those who believe in Him, and those who sincerely seek Him. It is impossible to

GOD'S Divine Understanding

please GOD without faith. GOD will reward those who are willing to "diligently seek" after Him.

[Heb 11:6 NKJV] But without faith [it is] impossible to please [Him], for he who comes to GOD must believe that He is, and [that] He is a rewarder of those who diligently seek Him.

Hebrews tells us it is impossible to please GOD without faith. So, it stands to reason you will need faith to search for Him. For it says, "anyone who wants to come to Him must believe that GOD exists". Therefore, the question becomes.... how do you believe in GOD, and what is faith?

[Heb 11:6 NLT] And it is impossible to please GOD without faith. Anyone who wants to come to him must believe that GOD exists....

[Heb 11:1, 3 NLT] Faith is the confidence that what we hope for will actually happen; it gives us assurance about things we cannot see. ... By faith we understand that the entire universe was formed at GOD's command, that what we now see did not come from anything that can be seen.

Faith is what brings us salvation. Faith is the foundation by which we have understanding. We cannot see GOD or touch Him but by faith we know Him and His love for us. GOD's love brings us to a relationship with Him. That is what faith is.... it is believing in what we cannot see and is something we cannot hold in our hand. To put it another way- now faith is the assurance of things hoped for, the conviction of things not seen:

[Heb 11:1-3 NIV] Now faith is confidence in what we hope for and assurance about what we

do not see. This is what the ancients were commended for. By faith we understand that the universe was formed at GOD's command, so that what is seen was not made out of what was visible.

Hebrews 11- tells us that faith in GOD is a sign of assurance that one is destined for the future Kingdom Of GOD. Faith is seen as a foundation to a house: It gives confidence and assurance that it will stand, faith is the assurance in GOD. The point of Faith is to connect us with GOD so that all of us can overcome our trials and obstacles. GOD has provided faith so we can believe in Him and have confidence and trust in Him! This is just some of what Hebrews 11 has to say about faith. I encourage the reader to take the time to read all of it.

We see in the story of Cain and Abel, that it was by faith, Abel offered to GOD a more acceptable sacrifice than Cain, through which he was commended as righteous. Abel was seen as righteous because of His faith, where Cain was not, this implies that Cain did not have faith.

It was because of Enoch's faith that he was taken up so that he did not see death. The story of Enoch says he was found no more because GOD had taken him. Now before he was taken he was commended as having pleased GOD, We understand from the Bible, that without faith it is impossible to please him, for whoever would draw near to GOD must believe that he exists and that he rewards those who seek him. By faith Noah, constructed an ark. By faith Abraham obeyed GOD.

[Heb 11:11, 17, 20, 23-24, 28-31 NLT] It was by faith that even Sarah was able to have a child, though she was barren and was too old. She believed that GOD would keep his promise. ...It was by faith that Abraham offered Isaac as a sacrifice when GOD was testing him. Abraham, who had received GOD's promises, was ready to sacrifice his only son, Isaac, ... It was by faith that Isaac promised blessings for the future to his sons, Jacob and Esau. ... It was by faith that Moses' parents hid him for three months when he was born. They saw that GOD had given them an unusual child, and they were not afraid to disobey the king's command. It was by faith that Moses, when he grew up, refused to be called the son of Pharaoh's daughter. ... It was by faith that Moses commanded the people of Israel to keep the Passover and to sprinkle blood on the doorposts so that the angel of death would not kill their firstborn sons. It was by faith that the people of Israel went right through the Red Sea as though they were on dry ground. But when the Egyptians tried to follow, they were all drowned. It was by faith that the people of Israel marched around Jericho for seven days, and the walls came crashing down. It was by faith that Rahab the prostitute was not destroyed with the people in her city who refused to obey GOD. For she had given a friendly welcome to the spies.

It has been said, faith is mysterious and difficult. This is true, at times our trials in life are hard on our faith which makes it difficult to have faith. If the tribulation we go through makes Divine Understanding hard to understand, what are we to do?

Having an understanding of the true meaning of your trials and tribulation in your life is more important than you might think or imagined. When you do not have understanding, you fail to grasp that GOD will use your trials for your good. The Bible teaches that GOD will purify, cleanse and refine you by the trails you go through.

[Dan 12:10 NLT] Many will be purified, cleansed, and refined by these trials. But the wicked will continue in their wickedness, and none of them will understand. Only those who are wise will know what it means.

Therefore, GOD will use a trial that you are going through, to teach you who you can be, which makes discovering your true self possible. On the surface you have a complete identity of who you are. But you go through a trail that wakes you up to the fact that you truly do not know yourself.

Why is it so hard for us to become the person we were meant to be? Why do we have to go through trials? Understand, it is because Satan has had a hand in it all. We go through some painful tribulation and realize the reason we went through it was that GOD was giving us a reason to find Him. Our life journeys can take us over troubled waters.

Now I need to make a point. GOD knows you; He knew you before the earth was created. He knew you before you were ever born. He knows what you are going to do ahead of time.

[Gal 1:15 NLT] But even before I was born, GOD chose me and called me by his marvelous grace. Then it pleased him

[Eph 1:4 NLT] Even before he made the world, GOD loved us and chose us in Christ to be holy and without fault in his eyes.

So why does GOD allow trouble to prove the genuineness of our faith? GOD knows if our faith is genuine. Someone once said, GOD has put down certain guidelines that give us an idea of why He permits trouble to come. But understand those guidelines are not for GOD'S edification, but ours. GOD allows trials for us to know whether our faith is genuine.

When ore is tested to prove it is gold or silver, an analyst will put it through some tests to determine whether it is genuine. Likewise, GOD allows trials for us to test our faith- to prove if it is genuine. It is for our edification and not His. He knows whether or not- if it is genuine, but sometimes we have doubts. The tests are for our benefit.

When tribulation hits your life, your faith will be put to the test. Will you trust GOD? Will you lean on Him rather than lean on your own understanding? GOD tests our faith so that we might know it is genuine.

Nevertheless, GOD wants us to understand our trials and tribulations, so that we will realize we do not have to do it alone or the hard way. However, GOD does use our journeys in life to reveal Himself to us. When we discover the truth about our trials in our lives it is always to complete our growth with GOD.

Trials, tests, tribulation and temptation, what is the difference? Does GOD allow all to come into our lives? Does GOD cause any of them in our lives? I have not run across a scripture that indicates that GOD places evil in our way in order to test us. There are many verses where it is allowed, but none where He actually places trials of tribulation in our paths.

Yes, GOD will test you, but not with evil ways. So when He tests anyone it is not for His benefit -to find out how we would react. He already knows that. It is for our benefit.

What benefit is that? Ultimately, it is the experience of evil, which believe it or not GOD created, and He allows us to experience it. We are supposed to experience evil; it is part of life. Whereby, we will ultimately give GOD the glory for His mercy and salvation.

[Isa 45:7 KJV] I form the light, and create darkness: I make peace, and create evil: I the LORD do all these [things].

Yes, we do go through trials and tribulations that GOD will use, but these trials and tribulations are from the choices we make, and do not come from GOD.

[Jas 1:12 NIV] Blessed is the one who perseveres under trial because, having stood

the test, that person will receive the crown of life that the Lord has promised to those who love him.

GOD will never ever temp you. All temptation comes from life where you are enticed by your own evil desire, and Satan the devil. The good news, GOD will not let you be tempted beyond what you can bear. And He will always provide a way out.

[1Co 10:13 NIV] No temptation has overtaken you except what is common to mankind. And GOD is faithful; he will not let you be tempted beyond what you can bear. But when you are tempted, he will also provide a way out so that you can endure it.

[Jas 1:13-14 NIV] When tempted, no one should say, "GOD is tempting me." For GOD cannot be tempted by evil, nor does he tempt anyone; but each person is tempted when they are dragged away by their own evil desire and enticed.

GOD has revealed His mysterious plan for us all. GOD has extended His Grace to all through the person of Jesus Christ. In addition, we all can share equally in the riches inherited through Jesus. In addition, we all can have understanding and insight into GOD's plan regarding Jesus Christ.

GOD's plan is for those who believe the Good News that the Christian Church preaches. All who believe the Good News will enjoy the promise of blessings because they are children of GOD and belong to Jesus Christ and put their faith in Him. All who believe in Jesus Christ will receive GOD'S gift of Salvation.

John Spiker,

[1Pe 1:5-7 NLT] And through your faith, GOD is protecting you by his power until you receive this salvation, which is ready to be revealed on the last day for all to see. So be truly glad. There is wonderful joy ahead, even though you have to endure many trials for a little while. These trials will show that your faith is genuine. It is being tested as fire tests and purifies gold--though your faith is far more precious than mere gold. So when your faith remains strong through many trials, it will bring you much praise and glory and honor on the day when Jesus Christ is revealed to the whole world.

The gospel of Jesus Christ is GOD's plan for our salvation through faith. It shows how through faith we can be saved. Faith and the Bible go hand in hand, the Bible teaches us how to have faith and in whom. Because of Jesus and our faith in Him, we can go boldly and confidently to GOD our father. GOD's eternal plan was to use the Church to reveal the Good News to the world and display His wisdom to all the unseen rulers and authorities in the heavenly places. The Good News is about GOD's wonderful Grace.....Jesus Christ and the Kingdom of GOD.

[Eph 3:8-12 NLT] Though I am the least deserving of all GOD's people, he graciously gave me the privilege of telling the Gentiles about the endless treasures available to them in Christ. I was chosen to explain to everyone this mysterious plan that GOD, the Creator of all

things, had kept secret from the beginning. GOD's purpose in all this was to use the church to display his wisdom in its rich variety to all the unseen rulers and authorities in the heavenly places. This was his eternal plan, which he carried out through Christ Jesus our Lord. Because of Christ and our faith in him, we can now come boldly and confidently into GOD's presence.

We understand from scriptures in the Bible that it was Abrahams's faith in GOD that he was found to be righteous and it was faith that brought him into a relationship with GOD.

[Gen 15:6 NLT] And Abram believed the LORD, and the LORD counted him as righteous because of his faith.

Therefore, do not think or declare that you are good enough to be saved, if you do- then what you are saying is that faith is useless and meaningless. However, we know that this is not true; nevertheless, by now we Christians know that faith is the key to GOD's promises and that anyone can know and understand faith, just ask GOD the Father for the truth.

The Bible teaches us that GOD's promises are a free gift, and we receive these gifts through our faith. You are certain to receive GOD promises if you have the kind of faith that Abraham had, Abraham is the father to all who believe. GOD has shown us his mysterious plan of faith through Jesus, and he used Abraham's life before he sent Jesus to show us.

This is the way it was with us before Christ came, we were like children; we were slaves to the basic spiritual principles of this world (Sin). However, when the right time came, GOD sent his Son Jesus Christ as our Lord and Saver, through faith in Him we are saved. Through faith in GOD, we can have a personal relationship with Him.

Before Jesus, GOD gave the Law of Moses. The Law of Moses (also called Old Testament Law, Mosaic Law, or just The Law) regulated almost every aspect of Hebrew life. The Ten Commandments are just part of the bigger law. The Ten Commandments are just the morals law and are just a small part of the bigger law.

There are many other parts of the bigger laws that define matters of religious practice and government. It regulated the army, criminal justice, commerce, property rights, slavery, sexual relations, marriage and social interactions. It required circumcision for males, animal sacrifices, and strict Sabbath observance.

It provided for the welfare of widows, orphans, the poor, foreigners, and domestic animals. Ceremonial rules divided animals into "clean" and "unclean" categories. Clean animals could be eaten; unclean animals could not.

It has been said that the Law was not given to all- only to the chosen people, the Israelites. People are fond-of-saying... the majority of people have no Law from GOD to keep. So that means they can do whatever they want and not sin.

Many say the Church today never had to keep GOD'S Law, as it was given solely to his chosen people, the Israelites. But this is false, the law was given to all- the Israelites were to be the guardians of the law. Until GOD sent Jesus Christ to fulfill the law.

[Mat 5:17 NKJV] "Do not think that I came to destroy the Law or the Prophets. I did not come to destroy but to fulfill.

If Jesus did not come to abolish the law, does that mean all the Old Testament laws still apply to us today? Yes and NO.... No, if you believe in Jesus, you live under faith, the Grace of GOD.

Yes, if you do not have faith. Because without faith you live under the law. Remember Jesus came to fulfill the law as a perfect sacrifice. We understand everyone breaks the law; sin is contrary to the law.

[1Jo 3:4 NLT] Everyone who sins is breaking GOD's law, for all sin is contrary to the law of GOD.

The moral law (the Ten Commandments) is the direct command of GOD, and it requires strict obedience. The moral law reveals the nature and will of GOD, and it still applies today. Jesus obeyed the moral law completely, Jesus did not sin, in Him is no sin.

[1Jo 3:5 HNV] You know that he was revealed to take away our sins, and in him is no sin.

Jesus did not abolish the moral and ethical laws that had been in effect from the time of Moses. He affirmed and expanded upon those principles.

They are still in effect today. Only we do not live under the law, but under GOD'S Grace.

We live by faith, the Grace of GOD, and not the law. But the law teaches us how to live like a Christian; this more or less is living a holy and spiritual life. The law was given to teach us how to live a holy and spiritual life. Now because of Jesus, we receive the Holy Spirit that teaches us how to live a Holy and Spiritual life. It is by GOD'S Grace we receive the Holy Spirit.

However, freedom from the Old Testament Law is not a license for Christians to relax their moral standards. The moral and ethical teachings of Jesus and His apostles call for even greater self-discipline than those of the Old Testament Laws. Christians should still look to the Old Testament scripture for moral and spiritual guidance.

Here are just a few things Jesus had to say about the law. You can see how hard it would be to live by the law.

[Mat 5:21-22, 27-28, 38-39 NIV] "You have heard that it was said to the people long ago, 'You shall not murder, and anyone who murders will be subject to judgment.' But I tell you that anyone who is angry with a brother or sister will be subject to judgment....... "You have heard that it was said, 'You shall not commit adultery.' But I tell you that anyone who looks at a woman lustfully has already committed adultery with her in his heart. ... "You have heard that it was said, 'Eye for eye, and tooth for tooth.' But I tell you, do not resist an evil person. If anyone slaps

you on the right cheek, turn to them the other cheek also.

Understand, GOD gave the law where no one is able to keep it perfectly. The Bible makes it clear... no one is justified before GOD by the law. It tells us the righteous will live by faith.

[Gal 3:11 CSB] Now it is clear that no one is justified before GOD by the law, because the righteous will live by faith.

The law is perfect, and to be fulfilled it required a perfect sacrifice-one having all the required elements, qualities, and characteristics of GOD, the righteousness of GOD.

Hence, Jesus Christ was the only one who could fulfill the law. The Law is the issue that must be dealt with in order to bring us into a right relationship with GOD. GOD and Jesus are far from the wicked. GOD sent Jesus Christ, so in Him, we might become the righteousness of GOD.

[Pro 15:29 NKJV] The LORD [is] far from the wicked, But He hears the prayer of the righteous.

[2Co 5:21 CSB] He made the one who did not know sin to be sin for us, so that in him we might become the righteousness of GOD.

As we now understand, Jesus came to fulfill the law, to be fulfilled, it had to be a perfect sacrifice. The Bible says all who try to live by the law are under a curse, because they must do everything written in the law. The curse is death.

[Gal 3:10 CSB] For all who rely on the works of the law are under a curse, because it is

written, Everyone who does not do everything written in the book of the law is cursed.

From the time of Moses until Jesus, the Scriptures teach us that people were slaves to sin. And from Adam to Moses people were not slaves to sin. People lived under a kind of grace...From Adam to Moses there was no law to live by.

Adam's fall caused him to sin by eating from the tree of knowledge of good and evil... Part of the human dilemma as a consequence of this fall is that humans have enormous knowledge of how to do bad things as well as how to do good things.

[Gen 2:16-17 NLT] But the LORD GOD warned him, "You may freely eat the fruit of every tree in the garden-- except the tree of the knowledge of good and evil. If you eat its fruit, you are sure to die."

So before Moses people knew if they were doing bad things, as well as good, even before the law. But Scriptures teach us the bad done was not counted as sin, because before Moses there was no law.

But at the same time, all sin is contrary to the law. In fact, sin was in the world before the law, but sin is not charged to a person's account when there was no law. There was sin in the world, in fact we now know sin brought a curse to all.

Nevertheless, death reigned from Adam to Moses, for everyone has sinned from the time of Adam. There was no law, but humans had knowledge of good and evil. But before Moses all bad done is not charged against them.

[Rom 5:12-14 NLT] When Adam sinned, sin entered the world. Adam's sin brought death, so death spread to everyone, for everyone sinned. Yes, people sinned even before the law was given. But it was not counted as sin because there was not yet any law to break. Still, everyone died--from the time of Adam to the time of Moses--even those who did not disobey an explicit commandment of GOD, as Adam did......

To summarize, from Adam till Moses sin was in the world. But sin was not counted as sin because GOD did not give the law as of yet. From Moses to Jesus Christ, people lived under the law. From the time of Jesus, people have lived under GOD'S Grace. If people chose not to live under GOD'S Grace, then they live under the law and are under a curse!

Jesus didn't come to free us from the Law. He came to free us from sin, the curse. He didn't need to free us from the Law because the Law never enslaved us in the first place. The curse enslaves. If anyone could keep all the law, there was no sin in them...Jesus lived a sinless life that's how He was able to fulfill the law. And that's how we know that a man is not justified by observing the law, but by faith in Jesus Christ.

The Law was part of what set the people of Israel apart. It made them distinct from all other nations and identified them as GOD's chosen people: The people of Israel were instructed in holiness the moment the Law was given, and this continues even today.

The trouble is no one is able to keep the law perfectly. GOD allowed for the atonement for sin in the existence of a sacrifice. Which was a perfect example of the grace of GOD revealed through the Law. People had to make sacrifices for the atonement for sin, before Jesus.

Being under the law is being guilty before GOD. In other words, those who are under the law are guilty of breaking it and are under the curse of it. Remember no one can keep the law, everyone is guilty of breaking the law before GOD.

By living under grace instead of the law, Christians are—not guilty and cursed by the law. Therefore, they do not live under a curse but, rather, are under the power and Grace of GOD instead.

[Rom 3:19-20 NLT] Obviously, the law applies to those to whom it was given, for its purpose is to keep people from having excuses, and to show that the entire world is guilty before GOD. For no one can ever be made right with GOD by doing what the law commands. The law simply shows us how sinful we are.

GOD made a New Covenant with anyone who believes. In this new covenant, the Law is written on the hearts of those who believe. Understand, sin is no longer your master, for you no longer live under the requirements of the law. Instead, you live under the freedom of GOD's Grace.

[Jer 31:31-34 NLT] "The day is coming," says the LORD, "when I will make a new covenant with the people of Israel and Judah.

This covenant will not be like the one I made with their ancestors when I took them by the hand and brought them out of the land of Egypt. They broke that covenant, though I loved them as a husband loves his wife," says the LORD. "But this is the new covenant I will make with the people of Israel on that day," says the LORD. "I will put my instructions deep within them, and I will write them on their hearts. I will be their GOD, and they will be my people. And they will not need to teach their neighbors, nor will they need to teach their relatives, saying, 'You should know the LORD.' For everyone, from the least to the greatest, will know me already," says the LORD. "And I will forgive their wickedness, and I will never again remember their sins.

Now before anyone wants to take me to task about who GOD made this New Covenant with! I am talking to you people, who say I was never under the law, and I can do what I want and still be saved. Because the covenant was with the people of Israel and Judah. People have often used this verse from Jeremiah, to justify many things, including sin.

Yes, the scripture does say; "when I will make a new covenant with the people of Israel and Judah". But to understand this you must know when and who GOD was talking to at the time. First, know this is from the Old Testament, meaning before Jesus. Meaning GOD had not yet revealed His mysterious plan.

GOD was talking to Jeremiah, a Hebrew prophet-at the time the Hebrews were under the control of the Babylonians and were in exile. GOD was telling Jeremiah what was to come of the Hebrew people. GOD made Jeremiah a promise of redemption to the people, as individuals rather than a Nation. And that promise was based on GOD'S grace rather than a person's adherence to the law.

At the time GOD had spoken to Jeremiah, Israel and Judah were divided into two separate nations. But GOD had promised that He would make this covenant with both houses. GOD references the Mosaic Covenant—a covenant that was conditioned on Israel's obedience. And you now understand no one could live under the law, they had to make atonement for sin in the existence of a sacrifice.

If you read the Books of the law, you will see several places where GOD shares the promises of blessing for Israel if they obey His law and promises of curses if they broke it. The Hebrew people broke the law, that's why they were in excel, it was part of GOD curse on the people of Israel and Judah. The new covenant was not conditional on the law.

We see where GOD made new promises, which are in the New Testament. (" Both Gentiles and Jews who believe the Good News share equally in the riches inherited by GOD'S children. Both are part of the same body, and both enjoy the promise of blessings".)

The point you need to understand, Jeremiah did not know of GOD'S mysterious plan, for GOD did not reveal it as of yet. It had been kept secret from the beginning. GOD's purpose in all this was to use the church to display his secret. This was his eternal plan, which he carried out through Jesus Christ our Lord.

Wherefore, we know that the new covenant centers on Jesus Christ. Jesus is the way that GOD has forgiven us for our wrongdoings. Understand it is through Israel that GOD has blessed all the nations of the world because of this new covenant.

Read what say scriptures say in Ephesians 3.... Where it says, "Both Gentiles and Jews who believe the Good News share equally in the riches inherited by GOD's children. Both are part of the same body, and both enjoy the promise of blessings because they belong to Christ Jesus".

Eph 3:3-6, 9-11 NLT] As I briefly wrote earlier, GOD himself revealed his mysterious plan to me. As you read what I have written, you will understand my insight into this plan regarding Christ. GOD did not reveal it to previous generations, but now by his Spirit he has revealed it to his holy apostles and prophets. And this is GOD's plan: Both Gentiles and Jews who believe the Good News share equally in the riches inherited by GOD's children. Both are part of the same body, and both enjoy the promise of blessings because they belong to Christ Jesus. ...

Understand, GOD Made a way to get right with Him without keeping the requirements of the law. By having faith in Jesus Christ. Remember people had to live by the law, they were placed under the guard of the law. The Bible says they were kept in protective custody until the way of faith was revealed, (GOD'S mysterious plan).

Now that the way of faith has come, we no longer need the law as our guardian. Because of Jesus Christ did away with the law so that there may be righteousness for everyone who believes

[Gal 2:16 NLT] Yet we know that a person is made right with GOD by faith in Jesus Christ, not by obeying the law. And we have believed in Christ Jesus, so that we might be made right with GOD because of our faith in Christ, not because we have obeyed the law. For no one will ever be made right with GOD by obeying the law."

[Rom 3:21 NLT] But now GOD has shown us a way to be made right with him without keeping the requirements of the law, as was promised in the writings of Moses and the prophets long ago.

[Rom 6:14 NLT] Sin is no longer your master, for you no longer live under the requirements of the law. Instead, you live under the freedom of GOD's grace.

[Gal 3:12, 19, 23, 25 NLT] This way of faith is very different from the way of law, which says, "It is through obeying the law that a person has life." ... Why, then, was the law given? It was given alongside the promise to show people their sins. But the law was designed to last only until the coming of the child who was promised. GOD gave his law

through angels to Moses, who was the mediator between GOD and the people. ... Before the way of faith in Christ was available to us, we were placed under guard by the law. We were kept in protective custody, so to speak, until the way of faith was revealed. ... And now that the way of faith has come, we no longer need the law as our guardian.

[Gal 4:4 NLT] But when the right time came, GOD sent his Son, born of a woman, subject to the law.

I do not want you to miss this, "GOD sent his Son, born of a woman, subject to the law." GOD'S mother, the Virgin Mary was subject to the law. Therefore, Jesus was also under the law. Now read what the scriptures say about this son born of a woman:

[Isa 9:6 NLT] For a child is born to us, a son is given to us. The government will rest on his shoulders. And he will be called: Wonderful Counselor, Mighty GOD, Everlasting Father, Prince of Peace.

Now that we have Jesus, we can all be saved no matter what we have done. We are made right in GOD'S sight when we believe His promise to take away our sins. All we must do is trust in Jesus, have faith in Him and call on His name. Divine Understanding teaches us that there is only one path that leads to GOD. And that path makes our sins go away, by faith in Jesus. Because of our faith in Jesus, we receive GOD'S approval.

Before moving on, I need to say something about the church and the law. People in the church ask...Are we still under the law? And is often asked in an effort to diminish the law of GOD in the life of the Christian. It is said, "Since we are not under law but under grace, we do not need to keep the "Ten Commandments" any longer.

The Bible certainly does say we are no longer under law, but under grace. But does that imply that we are free from the obligation to obey it? Some read this to mean they can break the law because they are under grace, and not the law. The Law of Moses regulated almost every aspect of life in Old Testament times.

But with the coming of Jesus, GOD established a new covenant of faith with mankind. Christians are not required to follow the Old Testament Laws. However, the moral and ethical teachings of Jesus and the ten Commandments call for even greater self-discipline than those of the Old Testament. Jesus said, the law will not disappear from us until everything is accomplished. But because of GOD'S grace we do not live under the law. But know that if you do not have faith in Jesus, you are under the law. And the law leads to death, that is the curse, death.

[Rom 6:15-16 NLT] Well then, since GOD's grace has set us free from the law, does that mean we can go on sinning? Of course not! Don't you realize that you become the slave of whatever you choose to obey? You can be a slave to sin, which leads to death, or you can choose to obey GOD, which leads to righteous living.

[Mat 5:18 NIV] For truly I tell you, until heaven and earth disappear, not the smallest letter, not the least stroke of a pen, will by any means disappear from the Law until everything is accomplished.

In the strongest possible language, Paul states that being under grace does not give a license to break the law. Yet this is what millions believe today, missing Paul's clear point. Therefore, if being under grace does not exempt us from keeping the law, then what does the Bible mean by, not under the law, but grace.

For no one can ever be made right with GOD by doing what the law commands. The law simply shows us how sinful we are. But now GOD has shown us a way to be made right with him without keeping the requirements of the law, as was promised in the writings of Moses and the prophets long ago. We are made right with GOD by placing our faith in Jesus Christ. And this is true for everyone who believes, no matter who we are.

What is Faith?

If we are made right with GOD by placing our faith in Jesus; Then what is faith? Faith is not a thing you can buy, like a piece of furniture, or an attitude you cultivate through positive thinking. Faith is believing in what GOD has promised, where positive thinking is something you do on your own merit. Positive thinking is useful, and even necessary in achieving faith, but not on your own merit. You first must seek GOD, not just think about Him.

Faith is much like learning to ride a bike, you have to acquire some skill first, before you can ride that bike well. Oh, you may fall a few times off that bike before you master the skills to ride. So too is faith, you may fall from your faith. But like that bike you get back on, so too with your faith.

You gain faith even though you fell off your bike, so you will gain faith in your trails. Did you wish you could ride that bike, no you had to climb on it and acquire the skills needed. Oh, how you might have wished you could ride that bike, but you had to get on it first.

Faith is not positive thinking or will power; you do not just conjure it up. Faith is a free gift from GOD, a perfect gift. With all gifts from GOD, you must ask for it. The light bulb makes no effort to come on until you hit the switch. Wishing for faith will not work, you must seek it.

Faith is a day-by-day situation that we must face. Life is of course full of problems, involving temptation, trails, suffering, forgiveness and more. Faith does not give any guarantees to an easy life, but it does guarantee an eternity.

Faith will begin for most of us in very small quantities. The mustard seed is the smallest of seeds but can grow to be a tree. It will not grow until it is planted, and the ground receives it, without nourishment it will not grow. This is faith, you must look for it and you must receive it, and you must give it nourishment, seeking the word of GOD.

Like yeast, faith will only take a little bit to permeate through you. Try exposing yourself to religion it can be contagious. Try reading the Bible; you will not catch faith if you do not give it a try. You will not be able to catch it by staying away from church, or the Bible.

Sitting in a church and going to places to hear about GOD is not enough either. It is essential that you ask GOD for faith and believe in faith. That way you will catch it. If you think that you cannot catch faith or that you could never have real faith all you have to do is just ask GOD.

By thinking you cannot have faith, is like twisting the tap off to shut off the water; and looking for it to come on again. It will not come on until you twist that tap back on. If you stop looking for faith, you surely won't find it. By twisting off that tap, you will be shutting yourself off from GOD and His will for you.

[2Co 13:5 CSB] Test yourselves to see if you are in the faith. Examine yourselves. Or do you yourselves not recognize that Jesus Christ is in you? -- unless you fail the test.

2 Corinthians above says we should test ourselves, examine ourselves to see if we are in the faith. If you know Jesus lives in you, you have faith. If you do not believe Jesus lives in you, you failed the test.

GOD will help if you really search for Him and believe that Jesus lives in all of us. I suggest you try taking a long hard look at yourself and be honest. Look to see if there is anything holding you back, anger, hatred, jealousy, resentment, fears, and guilt are just some of the things the devil will use to get in your way of faith. Test your faith.

It is important to surrender these faults to GOD. If you make a sincere effort you will find that a little faith will go a long way. You will not get rid of sin unless you get rid of your ways. This is what Jesus meant by being born again. You can have a new life and new goals with faith. You will be transformed into someone of faith and be born again.

[1Pe 1:3-5 NLT] All praise to GOD, the Father of our Lord Jesus Christ. It is by his great mercy that we have been born again, because GOD raised Jesus Christ from the dead. Now we live with great expectation, and we have a priceless inheritance--an inheritance that is kept in heaven for you, pure and undefiled, beyond the reach of change and decay. And through your faith, GOD is protecting you by his power until you receive this salvation, which is ready to be revealed on the last day for all to see.

As the Bible plainly says, we are made right by our faith. We cannot earn our salvation; that is impossible. It is a free gift from GOD our Father. As Abraham believed GOD He was justified by GOD and made righteous, so it is with us, if we believe what GOD says and we too will be justified.

One question that gets asked quite a bit.... how can you have faith? The source of all faith comes from GOD. Faith comes by hearing and understanding GOD. We acquire our faith by hearing the word of GOD. You ask, what is the word of GOD? The Bible of course, that is why we need to read and listen to what the scriptures are saying.

It is not enough to just hear the word to be justified but to do what the scriptures say. Practicing GOD's word is very important to our spiritual growth. Building up faith is a lot like building muscles, you must use them repeatedly, so it is with faith, hear it, read it, and use it. There will be times in your life that GOD will bring you into situations where you will have to exercise your faith to get through. These times will be very emotional for you, but the outcome will not be affected by the way you feel. It will absolutely have nothing to do with your emotions. You just have to put your trust in GOD, and He will take care of the problem.

Faith in GOD can move mountains, heal the sick, but to have that kind of faith, you must learn to trust Him with everything in your life. The Lord protects those of childlike faith, the child does not use principles of reasoning all the reasoning they need is what they were told. The child will accept without any proof or evidence what their Father or Mother says they have trust in what the parents say.

You will need to have faith like that child, faith in the Father in heaven and your faith is far more precious to GOD then mere gold. If your faith remains strong after all the trails you must go through it will bring you much praise and glory and honor on the day when Jesus Christ is revealed to the whole world. Your reward for trusting him with childlike faith will be the salvation of your soul.

[Psa 116:3-6 NLT] Death wrapped its ropes around me; the terrors of the grave overtook me. I saw only trouble and sorrow. Then I called on the name of the LORD: "Please, LORD, save

me!" How kind the LORD is! How good he is! So merciful, this GOD of ours! The LORD protects those of childlike faith; I was facing death, and he saved me.

In Psalms above, it says that a sinner was facing death and saw only trouble and sorrow. Jesus saved him because he became a believer with childlike faith. He was born again and was transformed into someone of faith.

We all face death that do evil, (sin) and then does not repent. If an evil sinner will repent, they may face physical death but not spiritual death (the soul). In addition, do not fear those who kill the body but cannot kill the soul; rather fear him who can destroy both soul and body in hell,

Faith is complete trust, confidence, and reliance in GOD. It is a firm belief without proof, a calling from the bottom of our heart for GOD's kingdom to come. It means absolute allegiance and loyalty to GOD no matter what the circumstances. Faith is not just knowing the truth or accepting the truth, but it is proclaiming the truth, rejoicing in the truth.

Most importantly, it means living the truth. To have faith is to exercise GOD's principle in every part of our life. It is not to put the knowledge of GOD to work. But to put us to work in GOD's knowledge. It is not just a momentary moment, but a life-long commitment and practice in every deed we do, to live in obedience.

To live in obedience means to actively obey GOD and submit our lives to Jesus Christ. True faith is the determination to be obedient to GOD in one's life. True faith always comes with a desire to do GOD's will. And to do GOD's will, will inevitably result in good works. We are justified by our faith, which inevitably produces good works.

Perfect faith and obedience do not appear overnight. Obedience, devotion, and putting GOD's principles to work are the result of spiritual growth and spiritual maturity. The more we know the truth, the more we can see the reality of GOD, and the stronger our faith will be. The better we know Christ, the closer we unite with Him, and the better we will stand in our time of trials.

Spiritual growth is essential to our salvation, because it is the only way to sustain our faith. Like all living things when they stop growing, they tend to die, so does our faith. We must exercise our faith and take personal responsibility to protect it from sin, if not it inevitable will die and go away.

[Gal 3:22-23 NLT] But the Scriptures declare that we are all prisoners of sin, so we receive GOD's promise of freedom only by believing in Jesus Christ. Before the way of faith in Christ was available to us, we were placed under guard by the law. We were kept in protective custody, so to speak, until the way of faith was revealed.

The truth is we live in a world controlled by Satan; there are all kinds of temptations around us. These temptations may come from the world, or from our own sinful nature. They can cause our faith to die. Our worldly desires, worries, and hardships influence our faith. Our negligence may cause it to wither and die.

Our faith can also be affected by false doctrines. If we do not watch carefully and work diligently to promote our faith to grow stronger and stronger, even though we are saved through our initial faith, we may lose our faith and lose our salvation in the end.

The Bible has made the meaning of Jesus Christ's death clear to us. Here is what Galatians has to say... Did you receive the Holy Spirit by obeying the law of Moses? Of course not! You received the Spirit because you believed the message you heard about Christ. So all who put their faith in Christ share the same blessing Abraham received because of his faith. The real children of Abraham, then, are those who put their faith in GOD.

[Gal 3:1-14 NLT] Oh, foolish Galatians! Who has cast an evil spell on you? For the meaning of Jesus Christ's death was made as clear to you as if you had seen a picture of his death on the cross. Let me ask you this one question: Did you receive the Holy Spirit by obeying the law of Moses? Of course not! You received the Spirit because you believed the message you heard about Christ. How foolish can you be? After starting your Christian lives in the Spirit, why are you now trying to become perfect by your own human effort? Have you experienced so much for nothing? Surely it was not in vain, was it? I ask you again, does GOD

give you the Holy Spirit and work miracles among you because you obey the law? Of course not! It is because you believe the message you heard about Christ. In the same way, "Abraham believed GOD, and GOD counted him as righteous because of his faith." The real children of Abraham, then, are those who put their faith in GOD. What's more, the Scriptures looked forward to this time when GOD would declare the Gentiles to be righteous because of their faith. GOD proclaimed this good news to Abraham long ago when he said, "All nations will be blessed through you." So all who put their faith in Christ share the same blessing Abraham received because of his faith. But those who depend on the law to make them right with GOD are under his curse, for the Scriptures say, "Cursed is everyone who does not observe and obey all the commands that are written in GOD's Book of the Law." So it is clear that no one can be made right with GOD by trying to keep the law. For the Scriptures say, "It is through faith that a righteous person has life." This way of faith is very different from the way of law, which says, "It is through obeying the law that a person has life." But Christ has rescued us from the curse pronounced by the law. When he was hung on the cross, he took upon himself the curse for our wrongdoing. For it is written in the Scriptures, "Cursed is everyone who is hung on a tree." Through Christ Jesus, GOD has blessed the Gentiles with the same blessing he promised to Abraham, so that we who are believers might receive the promised Holy Spirit through faith.

You have the choice to live in faith or not. GOD's grace does not nullify your freedom to choose or exempt us from bearing the consequence of our choice but gives us true freedom and power to exercise our free choice to unite with Him. We are able to exercise our free will in every choice we make, in every step, and in every deed, we do.

Every time we exercise that free choice, we either strengthen our connection to GOD or weaken it, and it will affect our salvation either positively or negatively.

We now understand that Spiritual reading invigorates us to have more faith and a desire for more of GOD'S why to live. If you do read the Bible or devotional books do not go too fast, you will want to digest and think on what it is you are taking in. I once read that it is not the bee that flies swiftly around from flower to flower that gathers the most honey, but the one that dives down deep into the flower that gets the most honey. And so, it is with your devotional reading, dive deep down into it and take your time, in this way you will gather the honey that is understanding.

The honey of understanding that I am talking about is...Jesus Christ. Jesus Christ is the foundation we put our trust in. He is what we can build our faith life on. Just as a good foundation is necessary to properly support a building. You need a good foundation to properly support your faith.

If the foundation of a building is not properly laid, the whole structure can collapse. The same is true with your faith. A wrong foundation will result in spiritual disaster. The right spiritual foundation is necessary to support the building of your faith life. Jesus stressed the need for building on a good spiritual foundation in the illustrated parable of The Wise and Foolish Builders.

[Mat 7:24-27 NIV] "Therefore everyone who hears these words of mine and puts them into practice is like a wise man who built his house on the rock. The rain came down, the streams rose, and the winds blew and beat against that house; yet it did not fall, because it had its foundation on the rock. But everyone who hears these words of mine and does not put them into practice is like a foolish man who built his house on sand. The rain came down, the streams rose, and the winds blew and beat against that house, and it fell with a great crash."

There are steps that are required for building and maturing in a good spiritual foundation, you must go to Jesus or call on Him, listen to what He has said and is saying to you, and you must take personal action on His teachings. It is not enough to do just one, but all are required to mature in your Christian walk.

A person can go to Jesus and hear what He has to say but not respond. You can know the word and still not act upon it. If Jesus is going to be the Lord of your life you must respond to His teachings.

The person who goes to Jesus and then acts on His word is called wise in scriptures.

Dig deep for your foundation making sure you are removing everything between you and the Rock, Jesus Christ your Lord and Saver. No one escapes the storms of life. Life's stormy circumstances are experienced by all. But what makes the difference is how people respond to them. On the right foundation, the storms cannot shake you.

So will the events of the end of this age strike you with hope and joy, or dread. As for me and my family, we will live with hope. Because of GOD'S mercy and glory, we have a living hope through the resurrection of Jesus Christ from the dead.

[1Pe 1:3 CSB] Blessed be the GOD and Father of our Lord Jesus Christ. Because of his great mercy he has given us new birth into a living hope through the resurrection of Jesus Christ from the dead.

Chapter 4
GOD'S Divine Understanding, Wisdom and Will for us.

Divine Understanding, the knowledge of truth is... Jesus Christ
paid a ransom for all. This is one of the first things we learned in the first chapter of this book. Because of that ransom we all can have the wisdom of GOD, and have His peace thereby have Divine Understanding.

[Jas 1:5 CSB] Now if any of you lacks wisdom, he should ask God -- who gives to all generously and ungrudgingly -- and it will be given to him.

It starts with the wisdom that Jesus Christ is our Lord and Saver, and that He is in our hearts. Thereby, if Jesus is in our hearts then you know that Jesus Christ is your Salvation, whereby you have Divine Understanding.

How can you know for sure, that Jesus is in your heart and that you believe and have faith? In chapter 5, we will go over how to pray to GOD, and ask GOD to come into your heart. For now, I will point out some ways we already know Jesus is in our hearts and you can tell if you have faith.

Remember in chapter 3 where in 2 Corinthians it said to test yourselves, to see if you are in the faith. If you recognize that Jesus is in you, in your heart. You pass the test of faith. You have faith and believe, you will need to just grow in your faith.

Also, I want you to remember from chapter 3 where in Jeremiah, God made a new covenant. God has made a New Covenant with anyone who believes. GOD has written on the hearts of those who believe. Therefore, it says if you will search for the Lord with all your heart, you will find Him. Also, you have faith if you can "Jesus is Lord," because no one can say that except by the Holy Spirit. And you now know that all believers have the Holy Spirit.

[Jer 29:13 CSB] "You will seek me and find me when you search for me with all your heart.

[1Co 12:3 CSB] Therefore I want you to know that no one speaking by the Spirit of God says, "Jesus is cursed," and no one can say, "Jesus is Lord," except by the Holy Spirit.

In John below we see where Jesus said, the believer will have living water flow from deep in them. He was talking about the Holy Spirit. Understand how the believes were going to receive the Spirit. Because Jesus had not paid that ransom yet and had not yet been glorified. Just proof that the Holy Spirit lives in all believers.

[Jhn 7:37-39 CSB] On the last and most important day of the festival, Jesus stood up and cried out, "If anyone is thirsty, let him come to me and drink. "The one who believes in me, as the Scripture has said, will have streams of living water flow from deep within him." He said

this about the Spirit. Those who believed in Jesus were going to receive the Spirit, for the Spirit had not yet been given because Jesus had not yet been glorified.

This is the wisdom of GOD; understanding Jesus lives in us all, with the Holy Spirit. if we invite them in. With that invite comes GOD'S Divine Understanding and Wisdom, they are written on our heart. Understand that if you invite GOD's understanding in it will come. And if you invite it in... you have passed the test.

The Bible makes it clear everyone knows GOD already. There are no excuses, everyone knows GOD, and everyone knows GOD'S instructions. The problem is some chose not to believe or invite GOD in.

An invite to GOD in essence is like a beacon that invites GOD'S Divine Understanding toward an ever-deeper connection with GOD and Jesus Christ. A beacon is designed to draw attention to a specific location. Like a lighthouse, which provides a way to navigate around obstacles. So to than GOD'S Divine Understanding and Wisdom will provide a way around your trials and tribulation, the obstacles of life.

When you have this wisdom and oneness with GOD you do not need to search outside yourself. We now understand that GOD is inside us all. With GOD in us, we have a desire to connect with Him.

The desire for that connection is the fuel that drives us to look for that wisdom and understanding. Therefore, it is the motivation to seek out help and guidance from GOD. Each and every individual can come to know this wisdom as Divine Understanding that is present within us all.

GOD'S Divine Understanding does not make life any easier for us. Nor does it make us rich or take away our trials. What it does is gives GOD'S peace in all our trials and tribulations and GOD'S Divine Understanding. Having Divine Understanding puts GOD'S peace in our hearts, and what is in our hearts is usually our nature.

The Bible says for us to store our treasures in Heaven, for where our treasures is, there our heart will be also. Therefore, by doing so our heart will be set on GOD. No one or anything will be able to destroy your treasure in heaven!

[Mat 6:19-21 NIV] "Do not store up for yourselves treasures on earth, where moths and vermin destroy, and where thieves break in and steal. But store up for yourselves treasures in heaven, where moths and vermin do not destroy, and where thieves do not break in and steal. For where your treasure is, there your heart will be also.

The Bible teaches that fools have a sinful nature and are always hostile to GOD. Let the Holy Spirit guide you, then you won't be foolish and do what your sinful nature craves. The Holy Spirit guides you to store your treasure up in heaven. We all have a sinful nature that comes from Adam and Eve.

[Rom 8:7 NLT] For the sinful nature is always hostile to GOD. It never did obey GOD's laws, and it never will.

[Gal 5:16 NLT] So I say, let the Holy Spirit guide your lives. Then you won't be doing what your sinful nature craves.

The Bible says fools have no interest in understanding, and that those who trust their own insight are foolish. That's their nature, they have no interest in understanding, they walk in their own foolish wisdom.

[Pro 18:2 NLT] Fools have no interest in understanding; they only want to air their own opinions.

[Pro 28:26 NLT] Those who trust their own insight are foolish, but anyone who walks in wisdom is safe.

A person's nature can be seen in their thoughts, as that person thinks.... so there are. A person is known by what is in their heart. Why is this? It is because the heart usually shows that person's nature. Moreover, you can tell what kind of person they are by their nature and you can tell if they have faith.

We can easily tell a bad person's heart, and we can reasonably presume a good person's heart. How can we do this? By looking at what they do and say. Their heart will always show their thoughts, and their thoughts will always be in what they do and say, their thoughts will be where their treasure is. We must keep in mind that our thoughts are just as important as what we say. GOD does know our thoughts; He knows what we are thinking. GOD'S peace will bring understanding and wisdom. Anybody can have GOD'S peace by seeking Him.

The Bible says anyone who walks in wisdom is safe.

Few realize how important to our spiritual life and the advancement in it is the cultivation of Divine Understanding in our thoughts and our hearts. As a rule, those who are living with GOD'S understanding in their thoughts and hearts will prosper in the Lord and grow in His peace, while those who have none, labor at a great disadvantage.

How do we cultivate this Divine Understanding? Think about it as if a person who does not relish a certain kind of food may learn to like it if they will persist in eating it. It is so with a person who does not have GOD'S understanding or a taste for it. They may come to enjoy it if they persist in their spiritual life.

GOD'S peace brings a state of tranquility and harmony in everything. In addition, you will have a personal relationship with GOD. With GOD'S Understanding you have order and security within your heart, freedom from discontent or oppressive thoughts and emotions.

That's not to say you will live a worry-free life, or not have tribulation in your life. Only that you will have an understanding of the things that worry you and the tribulation you go through. Remember we will all go through trials and tribulations, that is our sinful nature.

All of us have at times in our lives have been caught up by life's trials and tribulations. But understanding GOD in His fullness brings peace in everything.

I remember reading somewhere about some academic scholars who said understanding GOD in all His fullness would be impossible if He did exist. First, how would they know, fools have no interest in understanding. Fools have a sinful nature and are always hostile to GOD.

These scholars tried to quote the Bible to make their point, they pointed to Isaiah 55:8-9: Where it says, my thoughts are not your thoughts.

[Isa 55:8-9 KJV] For my thoughts [are] not your thoughts, neither [are] your ways my ways, saith the LORD. For [as] the heavens are higher than the earth, so are my ways higher than your ways, and my thoughts than your thoughts.

They pointed to: Job 36:26- where it says that GOD is infinitely beyond our understanding: **[Job 36:26 NLT] "Look, GOD is greater than we can understand. His years cannot be counted.**

And Romans 11:33- says; How unsearchable are his judgments, and his ways past tracing out: **[Rom 11:33 HNV] Oh the depth of the riches both of the wisdom and the knowledge of GOD! How unsearchable are his judgments, and his ways past tracing out!**

Therefore, I say to these scholars- they are in a place where they cannot know GOD. They lack wisdom. Maybe that is why they teach what they do, with their own understanding. The Bible tells us those who trust their insight are foolish. And that fools have no interest in understanding. They are only interested in their own opinion.

[Job 18:21 HNV] 21 Surely such are the dwellings of the unrighteous, This is the place of him who doesn't know GOD."

However, do the scriptures they quote mean we can't understand GOD and that we should avoid the subject altogether. No! Because the Bible has made many traits and attributes of GOD understandable. What they quoted are just attributes of GOD, the verse quoted do not say or mean we cannot know GOD.

Everyone can get to know GOD; all anyone has to do is seek Him. You can bet those scholars are not seeking GOD. Why would they, they have already said, He does not exist. As we understand you first have to seek Him to know Him.

We know that GOD has revealed Himself to us through the Bible. By reading and studying the Bible, we learn who He is, and how He has, and will respond to us. And we learn how He has revealed Himself to us.

Here are some of what the Bible has to say about GOD:

- GOD is addressed in parental terms, (Father).

- GOD is spirit and exists everywhere and knows everything.
- GOD exists in three Persons, the Father, Son, and Holy Spirit.
- GOD is infinite, and unchanging.
- GOD created the world and everything seen and unseen and He sustains it all.

- GOD is now fulfilling His eternal plan for the world in these end-times.
- GOD draws people to faith in Him, through His Son, Jesus.
- GOD will one day bring judgment to the world.

GOD'S attributes and characteristics, as revealed in the Bible: GOD is wisdom, and makes no mistakes. GOD knows everything, and His knowledge is infinite. GOD is without measure and infinite and knows no boundaries. GOD is in control of everything. There is absolutely no sin or evil in GOD, He is completely Holy. The Father, Son, and Holy Spirit are all called GOD, and giving worship the same. GOD is all powerful and Self-Existent, He has no beginning or end. GOD never changes. GOD, by nature, is inherently good. GOD is Gracious: GOD enjoys giving to those who love Him, even when they do not deserve it.

It is through GOD'S Divine Understanding that we know that we were redeemed, not with corruptible things of this world, useless ways of life handed down from our fathers, but with the precious blood of Jesus Christ.

Divine Understanding teaches us that GOD handpicked Jesus before He even laid the foundation of the world. And that GOD determined when He was going to reveal Jesus to us, in the end of times. And we know it was for our sake that He picked this time. So our faith and hope might be in GOD these last days.

Scripture tells us that we were united with Christ even before GOD made the world. It tells us how GOD decided in advance, to adopt us into his own family through Jesus Christ. And Scriptures tells us that GOD purchased our freedom with the blood of his Son and forgave our sins, through His Son Jesus Christ. This is wisdom and Divine Understanding.

[Eph 1:3-14 NLT] All praise to GOD, the Father of our Lord Jesus Christ, who has blessed us with every spiritual blessing in the heavenly realms because we are united with Christ. Even before he made the world, GOD loved us and chose us in Christ to be holy and without fault in his eyes. GOD decided in advance to adopt us into his own family by bringing us to himself through Jesus Christ. This is what he wanted to do, and it gave him great pleasure. So we praise GOD for the glorious grace he has poured out on us who belong to his dear Son. He is so rich in kindness and grace that he purchased our freedom with the blood of his Son and forgave our sins. He has showered his kindness on us, along with all wisdom and understanding. GOD has now revealed to us his mysterious plan regarding Christ, a plan to fulfill his own good pleasure. And this is the plan: At the right time he will bring everything together under the authority of Christ--everything in heaven and on earth. Furthermore, because we are united with Christ, we have received an inheritance from

GOD, for he chose us in advance, and he makes everything work out according to his plan. GOD'S purpose was that we Jews who were the first to trust in Christ would bring praise and glory to GOD. And now you Gentiles have also heard the truth, the Good News that GOD saves you. And when you believed in Christ, he identified you as his own by giving you the Holy Spirit, whom he promised long ago. The Spirit is GOD'S guarantee that he will give us the inheritance he promised and that he has purchased us to be his own people. He did this so we would praise and glorify him.

Remember no matter what life sends your way- you can face them with courage and hope through your faith. GOD'S peace and Divine Understanding comes from faith in Him. It all comes from a man who lived over two thousand years ago... Jesus Christ, have faith in Him and GOD will give you His Peace. Praise and glorify GOD, like the Bible says-this is just a small part of faith.

[Psa 86:12 KJV] 12 I will praise thee, O Lord my GOD, with all my heart: and I will glorify thy name for evermore.

Divine Understanding teaches us that GOD chose this time, the time we now live in, so we would seek Him. He has given us this Coronavirus pandemic so people all over the world above all else would seek the Kingdom Of GOD, before the end of time.

This pandemic, (The Coronavirus) that is storming around the world right now has people all over the world scared. Still, to say merely people are scared does not do it justice. Scared, is not strong enough to capture the fear people everywhere are feeling. The signs of alarm are everywhere; at least for those who have no Divine Understanding or clue to what is to come. Scriptures tell us not to be afraid.

[Luk 12:31-32 NLT] *Seek the Kingdom of GOD above all else, and he will give you everything you need. "So don't be afraid, little flock. Forit gives your Father great happiness to give you the Kingdom.*

Here is what you need to know. Jesus said, "be of good cheer." Fear not because He has overcome the world. **[Jhn 16:33 KJV]** *These things I have spoken unto you, that in me ye might have peace. In the world ye shall have tribulation: but be of good cheer; I have overcome the world.*

But fear not, in Jesus you can have peace. GOD is our refuge in ever-present trouble. **[Psa 46:1-2 NIV]** *....GOD is our refuge and strength, an ever-present help in trouble. Therefore we will not fear, though the earth give way and the mountains fall into the heart of the sea,*

How can we have hope and Divine Understanding if predictions of apocalyptic events lead to the collapse of civilization as we now know it? Or the destruction of the planet is at hand?

Hope comes from Divine Understand, and Divine Understanding comes from GOD. And we learn about GOD in the Bible. The Bible is your hope. We learn faith from the Bible. Seek GOD while He is near and there is still time.

Divine Understanding teaches us when everything is falling apart, we can have hope and rest in safety. There is a place where you could experience glorious safety, a place of peace, and joy: A place where you can have courage and experience GOD'S power and protection. All you have to do is devote your heart to GOD and pray to Him for Divine Understanding.

[Job 11:13-20 NIV] "Yet if you devote your heart to him and stretch out your hands to him, if you put away the sin that is in your hand and allow no evil to dwell in your tent, then, free of fault, you will lift up your face; you will stand firm and without fear. You will surely forget your trouble, recalling it only as waters gone by. Life will be brighter than noonday, and darkness will become like morning. You will be secure, because there is hope; you will look about you and take your rest in safety. You will lie down, with no one to make you afraid, and many will court your favor. But the eyes of the wicked will fail, and escape will elude them; their hope will become a dying gasp."

No matter what storm you're facing, like the Coronavirus: Jesus says, "I will give you rest." Though we may struggle with believing GOD has left us fending for ourselves in hard times, like the ones we are living in right now. There is good news, we're not alone-not ever. Everyone struggles with discouragement as they face the trials and sorrows of life.

[Jhn 16:33 NLT] I have told you all this so that you may have peace in me. Here on earth you will have many trials and sorrows. But take heart, because I have overcome the world."

Make no mistake, we all get down at times. We all go through life storms! Where do you go for hope when you are grieving, fearful or any other kind of storm in your life? Where do you go when you are confronted with the task of life, when everything around you is falling apart? Divine Understanding and GOD'S Wisdom teach us to go to the Lord Jesus Christ, for His yoke is easy and His burden is light.

[Mat 11:28-30 NIV] "Come to me, all you who are weary and burdened, and I will give you rest. Take my yoke upon you and learn from me, for I am gentle and humble in heart, and you will find rest for your souls. For my yoke is easy and my burden is light."

None of us are immune. Life is hard. And often there's not just one big thing, but just lots of little things that can drain us dry. The good news is we're not alone-not ever. Jesus left us His pace, so we would not be afraid of life.

[Jhn 14:27 NLT] "I am leaving you with a gift--peace of mind and heart. And the peace I give is a gift the world cannot give. So don't be troubled or afraid.

We receive GOD'S Divine Understanding and Wisdom, through prayer. And by seeking insight into Biblical Principles, by reading the Bible. The Bible says, Joyful is the person who finds wisdom, the one who gains understanding. Biblical Principles are found in Scriptures and teach us what we need to know about Divine Understanding and GOD'S Wisdom:

[Pro 3:13-21 NLT] Joyful is the person who finds wisdom, the one who gains understanding. For wisdom is more profitable than silver, and her wages are better than gold. Wisdom is more precious than rubies; nothing you desire can compare with her. She offers you long life in her right hand, and riches and honor in her left. She will guide you down delightful paths; all her ways are satisfying. Wisdom is a tree of life to those who embrace her; happy are those who hold her tightly. By wisdom the LORD founded the earth; by understanding he created the heavens. By his knowledge the deep fountains of the earth burst forth, and the dew settles beneath the night sky. My child, don't lose sight of common sense and discernment. Hang on to them,

Everyone can abide in hope and have courage in times of trouble. Everyone can be protected and rest in safety with GOD'S Divine Understanding. GOD'S Word gives us understanding on how He relates to us, His Creation. We learn Divine Understanding by examining GOD'S Word in depth. What Divine Understanding are you seeking in life- are you looking to be fulfilled? The majority of people would say a lot of different things, home/house, love, happiness, etc.: If we are being completely honest, few would say Divine Understanding of GOD!

When examining GOD'S Word found in the Holy Bible it explains to us that true fulfillment comes through a personal relationship with GOD the Father, Jesus Christ the Son, and the Holy Spirit. One theme of the Bible is that every person can be fulfilled and enter into GOD'S perfect plan and destiny for their lives through Divine Understanding.

I know we said it all before, but this is of extreme importance to grasp: Every person is to seek GOD and to establish an intimate, personal relationship with GOD the Father. Thereby, we understand that it is through Jesus that we have Salvation. If you stop and think about Divine Understanding and what is really important in this life. There are two special messages and revelations that jump out of the pages of the Bible.

The first special message and revelation is that everyone is to understand that Jesus Christ paid a heavy ransom with His life for us, so we could receive GOD'S gift of Salvation. Scriptures teach us that our salvation will be revealed to all on the last day. In other words, all will see who has received GOD Salvation and who has not on the last day.

[1Pe 1:5 NLT] And through your faith, GOD is protecting you by his power until you receive this salvation, which is ready to be revealed on the last day for all to see.

The second special message and revelation is that GOD the Father, His Son Jesus Christ, and His Holy Spirit are looking to establish and make a direct personal relationship with each person He has created.

Through Divine Understanding we see where our priorities should be in this life: We see that our priorities should be to search for GOD, and to seek GOD'S gift of Salvation. -If you seek GOD'S gift of Salvation, you will understand GOD'S will for you. You would be living with GOD'S Divine Understanding.

Furthermore, having Divine Understanding will help with uncertainty. It is a common experience with all that is going on in these times, to be uncertain about the future. It is not an exaggeration... to say that uncertainty has become a characteristic of our times.

If we pay attention to what the Bible says, and follow what the Bible tells us to do, we can be absolutely certain that we're doing the right thing, and we will have Divine Understanding. There would be a lot less uncertainty in our lives if we paid more attention to GOD'S Divine Understanding.

[Pro 2:2-11 HNV] So as to turn your ear to wisdom, And apply your heart to understanding; Yes, if you call out for discernment, And lift up your voice for understanding; If you seek her as silver, And search for her as for hidden treasures: Then you will understand the fear of the LORD, And find the knowledge of GOD. For the LORD gives wisdom. Out of his mouth comes knowledge and understanding. He lays up sound wisdom for the upright. He is a shield to those who walk in integrity; That he may guard the paths of justice, And preserve the way

of his holy ones. Then you will understand righteousness and justice, Equity and every good path. For wisdom will enter into your heart. Knowledge will be pleasant to your soul. Discretion will watch over you. Understanding will keep you,

Divine Understanding explains how GOD'S word says seek Him and He will give us rest. He does promise to fill us with the power of His Spirit and that His joy will be our strength in these uncertain times.

GOD reminds us that the battle is not ours but the Lord's. He does say that... "we wrestle not against flesh and blood, but against the spiritual forces of darkness in this life."

[Eph 6:12 KJV] For we wrestle not against flesh and blood, but against principalities, against powers, against the rulers of the darkness of this world, against spiritual wickedness in high [places].

We do not have to fear the battle with the rulers of darkness. If we have Divine Understanding. We know that GOD has blessed us with every spiritual blessing in heavenly realms.

Divine Understanding teaches us that GOD has poured His Grace out on us. And it teaches us that GOD is so rich in His kindness and Grace that he purchased our freedom with the blood of his Son and forgave our sins.

We understand that the forgiveness of our sins has great power over all evil and spiritual wickedness. Stop and give all glory and praise to

GOD the Father and thank Him for His Son Jesus Christ and the Holy Spirit.

Divine Understanding teaches us this is Wisdom: The wages of sin is death because all who sin live under the law. But Christians know and understand that Jesus Christ our Lord paid a ransom so we can have eternal life. Believers in Jesus know that if we confess with our mouth, "Jesus is Lord," and believe in our heart that GOD raised him from the dead, we will be saved. They also know that one believes with the heart, resulting in righteousness, and one confesses with the mouth, resulting in salvation.

[Rom 6:23 KJV] For the wages of sin [is] death; but the gift of GOD [is] eternal life through Jesus Christ our Lord.

[Rom 10:9-10 NIV] If you declare with your mouth, "Jesus is Lord," and believe in your heart that GOD raised him from the dead, you will be saved. For it is with your heart that you believe and are justified, and it is with your mouth that you profess your faith and are saved.

Where does wisdom come from? Where does understanding dwell? How can I know GOD'S Will? The fear of the Lord is the beginning of wisdom, wisdom equals understanding and by understanding you know GOD'S Will.

[Job 28:20, 23, 28 NIV] Where then does wisdom come from? Where does understanding dwell? ... GOD understands the way to it and he alone knows where it dwells, ... And he said to

the human race, "The fear of the Lord--that is wisdom, and to shun evil is understanding."

Where does wisdom come from? Where does understanding dwell? How can I know GOD'S Will?

[Psa 111:10 HNV] The fear of the LORD is the beginning of wisdom. All those who do his work have a good understanding.... "The fear of the Lord is the beginning of wisdom", are probably some of the most misunderstood words. Our minds go straight to the thought that the Lord is one to be scared of. But the truth is: To fear the Lord leads us to respect.

We learn how we are to act and even what we should say by fearing the Lord. Fear of the Lord gives us a healthy dose of dread, A great apprehension of fear. With this kind of fear, we will most likely repent from our sins. Repentance is the beginning of true wisdom. *"The fear of the Lord-- that is wisdom, and to shun evil is understanding."*

Believers should fear the consequences of their sins, therefore leading them to make wise decisions. To know GOD'S Will, we must forsake the wrong path. And get on the right path. Without the fear of consequence, one has a hard time getting on the right path.

The first step to getting on the path is to trust in the Lord with all your heart; do not depend on your own understanding; seek GOD'S Will and He will show you which path to take.

[Pro 3:5-6 NLT] Trust in the LORD with all your heart; do not depend on your own understanding. Seek his will in all you do, and he will show you which path to take.

Understand that fear of the Lord has nothing to do with being scared! It has everything to do with reverence and respect. Reverence is the feeling of deep respect.

To make a comparison: When a child misbehaves, the child may fear the consequences. But the Father corrects the child with love. Thereby, the child respects the father for the correction; And learns that the father is greater in knowledge and wisdom. Just like we need to learn that GOD is greater in knowledge and wisdom than we ever could be.

Where does wisdom come from? Where does understanding dwell? How can I know GOD'S Will? GOD'S Divine Understanding is knowing that Knowledge and Wisdom comes for GOD. And are far greater than we could ever imagine.

- It is fear of the Lord; This fear has nothing to do with being scared!

- It is seeing everything through GOD'S Divine Viewpoint.
- It is trusting in GOD with all your heart.
- It is understanding GOD'S timing.
- It is understanding why Jesus Christ died for us and much more.
- It is understanding GOD'S will for us.

Understanding God's Will:

The Bible tells us to turn our ear to wisdom, and to apply understanding, then we would understand the fear of the Lord, and find the knowledge of GOD and His will for us. You will never discover GOD'S will without the Bible, because GOD has given seven foundational instructions/plans for all mankind to live by. More in the next chapter on this.

The first step to understanding and applying GOD 'S will in our lives is to want to do his will. Everything we do can be an act of worship to GOD. Most of us at one time or another have asked, what is GOD" s Will for me? The ruling motive in our prayers should be that GOD'S will be accomplished, more on this in the next chapter.

Now there has been a lot written about this subject. And many Christians speak of knowing or doing GOD'S will, but what is it? I am going to try and answer that with what I believe is GOD'S perspective.

The Bible speaks of GOD'S will from more than one perspective. I want to focus on three.... our free will, GOD'S general will for us and GOD'S "Pleasing and Perfect Will."

What is free-will? We have free-will to choose. The power to make decisions on our own, rather than having GOD make them for us or predetermine what we do. GOD created humans in his image. Unlike animals, which act mainly on instinct, we resemble our Creator, we have free will.

We determine our future to a great extent through the choices we make. GOD does encourage us to make the right decision, but He lets us decide.

Understand, GOD'S will for us is to choose life. This is GOD'S "pleasing and perfect will." This offer of life would be meaningless, if it lacked free will. Instead of forcing us to do what he says, GOD warmly directs us in the way we should go, but we still get to choose.

There is a difference between the general will of God, and what is His ultimate plan for us, GOD'S Pleasing and Perfect Will". GOD'S Pleasing and Perfect Will is a specific purpose for each of us, and it relates to our future and hope for eternal life.

GOD'S pleasing and Perfect Will for us is that we should come to repentance, and not perish. In other words, His desire is for us to be saved from our sin!

[2Pe 3:9 CSB] ……..not wanting any to perish but all to come to repentance.

GOD'S General Will- directs us in our everyday lives. In most cases His general will, will not change our salvation. It is said that a man plans, but it is the Lord who determines their steps. (Through His General Will).

The Scriptures below says that GOD has a plan for our well-being, and future and a hope. This is GOD'S Pleasing and Perfect Will. The word "hope" here does not communicate uncertainty...Ie, as in you hope something might occur. But rather, it is a joyful assurance that GOD will extend His Salvation to us and that Jesus will return, Jesus is our hop. The future is an eternity with GOD. And that eternity is our well-being!

[Jer 29:11 CSB] "For I know the plans I have for you" -- this is the LORD's declaration -- "plans for your well-being, not for disaster, to give you a future and a hope.

Jesus return should have the believer living a godly life in an ungodly world. Titus says we are instructed to live righteous lives and devotion to GOD while we look forward with hope to that wonderful day Jesus will be revealed. This means that the believer should live each day in continual anticipation and expectation with the conviction that Jesus will come at any time.

[Tit 2:12-13 NLT] And we are instructed to turn from godless living and sinful pleasures. We should live in this evil world with wisdom, righteousness, and devotion to God, while we look forward with hope to that wonderful day when the glory of our great God and Savior, Jesus Christ, will be revealed.

The will of GOD- ("Pleasing and Perfect Will") is the fact that GOD has a perfect plan for all people. This is the greatest discovery we will ever make – GOD has a purpose and perfect plan for each human past, present and future. A plan for hope, our well-being, and future. He has a purpose for each of us...to have Salvation. GOD wants to intercede for us. It is His will that we should come to repentance, and not perish.

[Heb 7:25 CSB] Therefore, he is able to save completely those who come to God through him, since he always lives to intercede for them.

The Bible teaches us that we must be renewed by the Holy Spirit. So we can find GOD'S, "pleasing and perfect will. Which we now know GOD wants us to choose life, salvation and not perish to have a future.

[Rom 12:2 CSB] Do not be conformed to this age, but be transformed by the renewing of your mind, so that you may discern what is the good, pleasing, and perfect will of God.

What is GOD'S general will?

GOD'S General Will, an all-encompassing will for people. It is His specific will for each individual. GOD'S General will, is the sovereignty of GOD. It is what GOD wants for us, what He desires us to do.

In other words, the sovereignty of GOD is that He is the supreme authority and has all the power and all things are under His control. Under His Supreme Will. But through His Supreme Will, He gives us free-will choose.

Make no mistake, He has all the power, you may choose, but He may not agree with you. His will be done, if He so chooses, your free will is only for you to choose life or death, everything else is under GOD'S sovereignty, His power.

It is through GOD'S General Will, that He gives us a desire and purpose in life. Through many different gifts. He may desire you to be a doctor, or something else. He will encourage you to make the right decision. He will give you all the gifts you need to be a doctor. But do not forget you make that decision. As scripture says, you plan your ways, but it is GOD'S will that directs your steps.

[Pro 16:9 NKJV] A man's heart plans his way, But the LORD directs his steps.

Scripture teaches us we need GOD to direct our steps because we cannot understand our own way. GOD will show us which path to take, but we still have free-will to choose which path we take.

[Pro 20:24 NIV] A person's steps are directed by the LORD. How then can anyone understand their own way?

To summarize, through free-will we choose which path to take, but it is GOD'S Will that directs our steps. However often we do not choose GOD'S general will, or His pleasing and perfect will for us.

1 Thessalonians 5:16-18 tells us how to apply God's will to our lives: "Rejoice always, pray continually, give thanks in all circumstances; for this is GOD'S will for you. This is part of GOD'S Pleasing and Perfect Will. Micah 6 tells us GOD has told all of us all what is good and what He requires of His will.

[1Th 5:16-18 CSB] Rejoice always, pray constantly, give thanks in everything; for this is God's will for you in Christ Jesus.

[Mic 6:8 CSB] Mankind, he has told each of you what is good and what it is the LORD requires of you: to act justly, to love faithfulness, and to walk humbly with your God.

Having the will of GOD in your life means to submit your life to his will. It means laying down your dreams, desires, and wants because you would rather see his will and purpose happen instead of your own. GOD'S will for our lives has reason and purpose. 1 Timothy, says GOD "wants everyone to be saved and to understand the truth."

It is through scripture, where we can find meaning and principles discerning GOD'S will.

[1Pe 2:15 NIV] For it is God's will that by doing good you should silence the ignorant talk of foolish people.

[Eph 5:17, 20 NIV] Therefore do not be foolish, but understand what the Lord's will is. ... always giving thanks to God the Father for everything, in the name of our Lord Jesus Christ.

[Heb 10:36 CSB] For you need endurance, so that after you have done God's will, you may receive what was promised.

Scriptures teach us that GOD works out everything with the purpose of His will for our individual lives. This is GOD'S general Will at work. GOD is the One who works out everything in conformity with the purpose of his will, but we still have free-will. Deuteronomy says GOD has given us a choice between life and death.

[Eph 1:11 NIV] In him we were also chosen, having been predestined according to the plan of him who works out everything in conformity with the purpose of his will.

[Deu 30:19 NLT] "Today I have given you the choice between life and death, between blessings and curses. Now I call on heaven and earth to witness the choice you make. Oh, that you would choose life, so that you and your descendants might live!

The work of the Holy Spirit first begins in the understanding of GOD'S will. And the work of the Holy Spirit is carried on to our will, till there is a change of the whole man into the likeness of GOD, in knowledge, and righteousness, and holiness. GOD desires for all to be saved and come to the knowledge of the truth. The knowledge of truth...Is Jesus Christ paid a ransom for all.

[1Ti 2:3-6 NKJV] For this [is] good and acceptable in the sight of GOD our Savior, who desires all men to be saved and to come to the knowledge of the truth. For [there is] one GOD and one Mediator between GOD and men, [the] Man Christ Jesus, who gave Himself a ransom for all, to be testified in due time,

Chapter 5
Prayer and Fasting

[1Pe 4:7 NASB] The end of all things is near; therefore, be of sound judgment and sober [spirit] for the purpose of prayer.

Prayer and fasting are defined as voluntarily going without food in order to focus on prayer and fellowship with GOD. Prayer and fasting often go hand in hand, but this is not always the case. You can pray without fasting, and fast without prayer. It is when these two activities are combined and dedicated to GOD'S glory that they reach their full effectiveness.

Both the Old Testament and New Testament teach the value of fasting, and prayer, which is abstaining from food or drink in order to focus on prayer and seeking GOD'S Will. One of the most important things we can pray for someone is for them to know GOD'S will.

It has been said that one the greatest calling for a believer is to know GOD'S will and do it. We see in Colossians 1:9, that Paul prayed for the church in Colossae to know the will of GOD and be filled with all wisdom.

[Col 1:9 CSB] For this reason also, since the day we heard this, we haven't stopped praying for you. We are asking that you may be filled with the knowledge of his will in all wisdom and spiritual understanding.

Ephesians 5 says by wise and make the most of every opportunity. It says do not be foolish but understand what the Lord's will is.

[Eph 5:15-17 CSB] Pay careful attention, then, to how you live -- not as unwise people but as wise -- making the most of the time, because the days are evil. So don't be foolish, but understand what the Lord's will is.

Through many examples of people in the Bible who fasted and prayed, we can know that GOD grants supernatural revelation and wisdom through this practice, of praying His Will, and fasting.

Scripture tells us that fasting, and prayer will help us grow in a more intimate relationship with GOD and will open our eyes to what He wants to teach us and His will for us.

[Phl 4:4-7 NLT] Always be full of joy in the Lord. I say it again--rejoice! Let everyone see that you are considerate in all you do. Remember, the Lord is coming soon. Don't worry about anything; instead, pray about everything. Tell God what you need, and thank him for all he has done. Then you will experience God's peace, which exceeds anything we can understand. His peace will guard your hearts and minds as you live in Christ Jesus.

All right since you can pray without fasting, and fast without prayer. We start with what is prayer. Billy Graham answered the question about what prayer is this way: "Prayer is spiritual communication between man and GOD, a two-way relationship in which man should not only talk to GOD but also listen to Him".

Prayer, simply put, is conversing with GOD. Prayer is our direct line with heaven. Prayer is a communication process that allows us to talk to GOD! We now understand that GOD wants a one on one communication with each and everyone of us. Prayer is a device we use, it is necessary to communicate with GOD. It is much like when we use phones to talk to someone.

How do I start learning how to pray? There are no magical formulas, no specific format, or special time to pray. Prayer is having a conversation with GOD about anything, everything, anytime, and anywhere. Payer is talking to GOD, it's that simple.

If we look to the past, we know that prayer was immensely important to the believers of the past. Prayer is not a mysterious practice reserved only for the devoutly religious. It is simply communicating with GOD...listening and talking to Him. Sometimes it is spontaneous and in your own words. You do not need to be impressive with big words.

Our prayers being answered is not based on the fluency of our prayers. We don't have to use certain words or phrases to get GOD to answer our prayers. In fact, Jesus rebukes those who pray using repetitions prayers and babble. Babble in the dictionary-talk rapidly and continuously in a foolish, excited, or incomprehensible way.

***[Mat 6:5-8 NLT]** "When you pray, don't be like the hypocrites who love to pray publicly on street corners and in the synagogues where everyone can see them. I tell you the truth, that is all the reward they will ever get. But when you pray, go away by yourself, shut the door behind you, and pray to your Father in private. Then your Father, who sees everything, will reward you. "When you pray, don't babble on and on as people of other religions do. They think their prayers are answered merely by repeating their words again and again. Don't be like them, for your Father knows exactly what you need even before you ask him!*

Don't misunderstand what I am saying, GOD hears the prayers of the righteous. But most prayers given in this manner are not from the heart, they are not the earnest prayers that GOD seeks.

Understand, GOD'S power of prayers is available through all kinds of prayers. As long as they are in line with His will, and are earnest and given with thanksgiving, you can ask all kinds of requests. Present your requests to GOD, and the peace of GOD, which transcends all understanding, will guard your hearts and your minds.

Pray can be recited from memory or read from the Bible or a book. Prayer is basically talking

with GOD. You are simply expressing with your words what your heart desires.

You give thanks to GOD through prayer, and you are spending valuable time with Him. GOD wants us to take any concerns to Him in prayer, and GOD will act upon it according to His will. The Scriptures say if we ask anything according to the will of GOD, He hears our prayers.

[1Jo 5:14-15 NIV] **This is the confidence we have in approaching GOD: that if we ask anything according to his will, he hears us. And if we know that he hears us--whatever we ask--we know that we have what we asked of him.**

Don't misunderstand me; this does not mean GOD will give you everything you ask of Him: We aren't to pray foolishly or selfishly, or for anything GOD has forbidden. But the closer we get to GOD in prayer, the more sensitive we'll become to His will. But how do you know if you are praying according to GOD'S will?

First, if it concerns you it concerns Him...and His will for you! Scriptures say, "don't worry about anything, but in everything, through prayer and petition with thanksgiving, present your requests to GOD". This is GOD'S will- that we take everything to Him. Understand by taking all your concerns to GOD...you are doing His will.

One of our greatest privileges as believers is prayer, and GOD wants us to bring all our requests and concerns to Him, no matter what they are. He loves us, and anything that concerns us is a concern to Him. Our aim should be to bring glory to GOD in everything, that is GOD'S will.

Ok, you can see that if we bring all our concerns to GOD in prayer, we are doing His will. It really is that easy, no magic needed. No mysterious practice needed to know and do GOD'S will.

[Phl 4:6-7 CSB] Don't worry about anything, but in everything, through prayer and petition with thanksgiving, present your requests to GOD. ......

[1Co 10:31 NLT] So whether you eat or drink, or whatever you do, do it all for the glory of GOD.

Scriptures are full of godly people who prayer according to the will of GOD. Follow the examples of these godly people: Paul prayed for the salvation of Israel. David prayed for mercy and forgiveness when he sinned. The early church prayed for boldness to witness and to help others to come to GOD.

These prayers were according to the will of GOD, and similar prayers today can be as well. As with Paul and the early church, we should always be praying for the salvation of others. For ourselves, we should pray as David prayed, always aware of our sin and bringing it before GOD. David prayed in Psalm 143:10, "Teach me to do your will" The problem with most of us is not that we do not know GOD'S will, but that we do not follow His will.

[Psa 143:10 NLT] Teach me to do your will, for you are my God. May your gracious Spirit lead me forward on a firm footing.

Understanding sin can hinder our relationship with GOD and thwarts our prayers. Pray with the right motivation. Selfish motives will not be blessed by GOD. When you ask, you do not receive, because you ask with wrong motives.

[Jas 4:3 NLT] And even when you ask, you don't get it because your motives are all wrong-- you want only what will give you pleasure.

GOD delights in our prayers, and He wants us to bring our concerns and requests to Him. But He loves us and knows what is best for us, and He can be trusted to give us only what is right.

Prayer takes a whole new meaning when we realize that Prayer strengthens not only our faith, but our relationship with GOD. The only key to an effective prayer is prayer itself. By prayer we remain in GOD, our thoughts are on GOD.

[Jhn 15:4 CSB] "Remain in me, and I in you. Just as a branch is unable to produce fruit by itself unless it remains on the vine, neither can you unless you remain in me.

You want your prayers to be a natural part of your relationship with GOD. You should be very comfortable going to Him with all your needs and any concerns and give thanks to Him. And pray in His will. But people still struggle with the idea of praying according to the will of GOD.

This seems like such a wide-open promise.... Pray according to the will of GOD and your prayers will be answered. So why can't we simply ask—and expect to receive positive answers—when we pray about something that is GOD'S will?

We can expect to receive positive answers, 1 John 5:14-15 couldn't be clearer: "since we know

He hears us when we make our requests, we also know that He will give us what we ask for".

But we need first to answer the question: What is meant by "His will"? If we can grow in our understanding of the various ways that the Bible speaks about the will of GOD, it may help us figure out how to resolve this legitimate and practical question in our prayer life. We went over GOD'S Will in chapter 4, if you still do not understand, go back and read it again.

Let's try to answer it another way. GOD answers prayers of the believer, because they have faith. And are in a relationship with Him. The believer wants to follow GOD and actually listens to what He has to say. When the believer prays for anything, it is a natural part of their relationship with GOD.

So, why doesn't GOD answer everyone's prayers? I do not have all the answers, but it may be because they don't have a relationship with GOD. They may know that GOD exists, and they might even worship GOD from time to time. But those who never seem to have their prayers answered probably don't have a relationship with him. The better the relationship with GOD, the better your prayers will be answered.

And sometimes it takes a long time for prayers to be answered. It is not that GOD has said no. Sometimes the person has never received from GOD complete forgiveness for their sin. You see our sin, iniquities separate us from GOD.

[Isa 59:2 CSB] But your iniquities are separating you from your GOD, and your sins have hidden his face from you so that he does not listen.

When you have faith in GOD, you are a child of GOD. When you belong to GOD, He hears your prayers. If you know GOD listen to His voice. Jesus said, "I am the good shepherd. I know my sheep and my sheep know me...my sheep listen to my voice. I know them and they follow me".

It all comes down too, do you really know GOD, and does GOD know you? Do you have a relationship with him that warrants GOD answering your prayers? Or, is GOD just- pretty much a concept in your life? If you're not sure that you know GOD, you can begin a relationship with him right now!

Many people ask, since I know that some things are clearly according to GOD'S will, why can't I just pray directly about those things and know for certain that they're going to happen? Stop. They asked the question with dough, "and know for certain"? Get rid of all dough. We must ask in faith without doubting. Stop making this more complicated than it has to be.

[Jas 1:6-8 CSB] But let him ask in faith without doubting. For the doubter is like the surging sea, driven and tossed by the wind. That person should not expect to receive anything from the Lord, being double-minded and unstable in all his ways.

Certainly, people get sick, even die; financial problems are real, and all sorts of very difficult situations can come up. What then, how can prayer help?

    We have learned that the Bible tells us to give our concerns to GOD. Even as the situation remains dismal. The circumstances may look out of control, but they aren't. When the whole world seems to be falling apart, like it is today. GOD can keep everything together. This is when a person can be very grateful that they know GOD.

    GOD can provide solutions to the problem way beyond what you imagined possible. But if the circumstances do not improve, GOD can still give us his peace in the midst of it, while we wait. Sometimes we have to wait. It is at this point (when circumstances are still tough) that GOD asks us to continue to trust him -- to "walk by faith, not by sight" the But understand it's not blind faith; It is based on the very character of GOD.

    [Lam 3:25-26 CSB] *The LORD is good to those who wait for him, to the person who seeks him. It is good to wait quietly for salvation from the LORD.*

    [Psa 130:5 CSB] *I wait for the LORD; I wait and put my hope in his word.*

    [Isa 30:18 CSB] *18 Therefore the LORD is waiting to show you mercy, and is rising up to show you compassion, for the LORD is a just God. All who wait patiently for him are happy.*

    [Isa 33:2 CSB] *2 LORD, be gracious to us! We wait for you. Be our strength every morning and our salvation in time of trouble.*

In Summary: GOD does answer the prayers of his children (those who have received Him into their lives and seek to follow him). He asks us to take any concerns to him in prayer and he will act upon it according to his will. As we deal with difficulties, we are to cast our cares on Him. The basis for our hope and faith is the character of GOD. The better we know Him, the more apt we are to trust Him and have Him answer all prayers.

We should never ask GOD to do something out of His character; it will do us no good to do so. GOD our Father does not hide His character from us it is the same, as Jesus Christ and we know Jesus Christ's character very well.

We can learn the ways of GOD'S heart Jesus showed us all how to please GOD. Be patient and trust that the Lord will bring forth good in all that you do and in any situation. You are to remain faithful looking for direction and learning the ways and will of GOD.

Sometimes GOD will bring instant and immediate answers to our prayers, but most of the time you will have to be persistent and consistent in your prayers. You will need to do your part. You have probably heard GOD helps those who help themselves.

But this cannot be found anywhere in scripture, at least I have not found it. GOD is willing to help us, He only asks us to do our part and asks us to pray. Our prayers are answered according to the will of GOD.

Therefore, every prayer we pray or ask of GOD is not answered in the way we would like or wish. They are answered in accordance to His will. This is very confusing, why would GOD refuse to answer anything we request of Him. I definitely do not have all the answers, but you must remain in a relationship with the Lord. Even when the answer to your request appears to be utter silence or just plain no or you may have to wait for the right time.

[Isa 30:18 CSB] *Therefore the LORD is waiting to show you mercy, and is rising up to show you compassion, for the LORD is a just God. All who wait patiently for him are happy.*

Waiting is one of the most difficult parts or obstacles to a real relationship with GOD. Disappointment, frustration, confusion are natural responses to waiting on the GOD And worse yet when lives continue to be shattered and prayers seem to fall on death ears, it does feel like you have nowhere to go.

[Mic 7:7 CSB] *But I will look to the LORD; I will wait for the God of my salvation. My God will hear me.*

[Rom 8:25 CSB] *Now if we hope for what we do not see, we eagerly wait for it with patience.*

[1Co 1:7 CSB] *so that you do not lack any spiritual gift as you eagerly wait for the revelation of our Lord Jesus Christ.*

However, those who learned to wait and leave it in GOD'S hands and press on through those emotions develop a good working relationship with GOD. They find victory in their prayers.

[Psa 34:15 KJV] The eyes of the LORD [are] upon the righteous, and his ears [are open] unto their cry.

[Psa 145:18-19 NLT] The LORD is close to all who call on him, yes, to all who call on him in truth. He grants the desires of those who fear him; he hears their cries for help and rescues them.

To many people, prayer seems complicated, but it is simply talking to GOD. Here are some points about what prayer is: Prayer is important because it makes us righteous and more like Jesus. Because it reveals the heart and mind of GOD and His character along with His will for us.

The Lord hears the prayer of the righteous. Righteousness is the perfect holiness of Jesus Christ. Righteousness is an essential attribute to the character of GOD. Jesus is the one who did not sin. In Him we become the righteousness of GOD! The righteous will live by faith, and prayer show we have faith.

[Pro 15:29 NKJV] The LORD [is] far from the wicked, But He hears the prayer of the righteous.

[2Co 5:21 CSB] He made the one who did not know sin to be sin for us, so that in him we might become the righteousness of GOD.

[Jas 5:16 NLT] Confess your sins to each other and pray for each other so that you may be healed. The earnest prayer of a righteous person has great power and produces wonderful results.

[Rom 1:17 CSB] For in it the righteousness of GOD is revealed from faith to faith, just as it is written: The righteous will live by faith.

[Rom 5:1 CSB] Therefore, since we have been declared righteous by faith, we have peace with GOD through our Lord Jesus Christ.

Pray for the things for which the Bible commands prayer. We are told to pray: For our enemies: *[Mat 5:44 CSB] "But I tell you, love your enemies and pray for those who persecute you,*

For GOD to send missionaries: *[Luk 10:2 CSB] He told them, "The harvest is abundant, but the workers are few. Therefore, pray to the Lord of the harvest to send out workers into his harvest.*

So that you do not enter temptation: *[Mat 26:41 CSB] "Stay awake and pray, so that you won't enter into temptation. The spirit is willing, but the flesh is weak."*

For government authorities: *[1Ti 2:1-2 CSB] First of all, then, I urge that petitions, prayers, intercessions, and thanksgivings be made for everyone, for kings and all those who are in authority, so that we may lead a tranquil and quiet life in all GOD liness and dignity.*

For relief from affliction: *[Jas 5:13-15 CSB] Is anyone among you suffering? He should pray. Is anyone cheerful? He should sing praises. Is anyone among you sick? He should call for the elders of the church, and they are to pray over him, anointing him with oil in the name of the Lord. The prayer of faith will save the sick person, and the Lord will raise him up; if he has committed sins, he will be forgiven.*

Where GOD commands prayer, we can pray with confidence that we are praying according to His will. The above were prayers in GOD Will, there are more but I believe you get the point I was trying to make.

We saw in chapter 4 where we were to ask GOD for wisdom. So, praying according to the will of GOD includes asking for wisdom. We ask GOD in faith, that's how we know the will of GOD, through faith.

Asking in faith- is trusting in GOD. We must also trust that GOD is gracious and willing to answer our prayers: But when we ask, we must believe and have no doubt:

[Jas 1:6-7 CSB] But let him ask in faith without doubting. For the doubter is like the surging sea, driven and tossed by the wind. That person should not expect to receive anything from the Lord,

GOD desires for you to rely on Him at all times, in the good times as well as the bad. The basis of our prayers lies in the hope and faith we have in the character of GOD. The better we know His character the more we are to trust in Him. Understand that GOD, does take great joy when we trust in His integrity and character. He likes it when we make time to spend with Him, and He enjoys it when we are able to hear Him, and actually listen for Him. Our goal should be to get to know GOD'S ways and the best way to do this is by spending time with Him in prayer and reading and listening to His word.

[1Ti 2:1 CSB] First of all, then, I urge that petitions, prayers, intercessions, and thanksgivings be made for everyone,

You will know with confidence that GOD can hear you when you pray, so open that line of communication! Pray, knowing that no matter how far you roam, your connection with Him can never be lost!

The Will of GOD can be seen in Philippians:

[Phl 1:9-10 NLT] I pray that your love will overflow more and more, and that you will keep on growing in knowledge and understanding. For I want you to understand what really matters, so that you may live pure and blameless lives until the day of Christ's return.

Pray with a spirit of forgiveness toward others. A spirit of bitterness, anger, revenge or hatred toward others will prevent our hearts from praying in total submission to GOD.

[Mar 11:24-25 NLT] I tell you, you can pray for anything, and if you believe that you've received it, it will be yours. But when you are praying, first forgive anyone you are holding a grudge against, so that your Father in heaven will forgive your sins, too."

Scriptures teach us not to give offerings to GOD while there is conflict between ourselves and another person. It is like that with our prayers, GOD does not want the offering of our prayers until we have reconciled with our brothers and sisters in Christ.

[Mat 5:23-24 NIV] "Therefore, if you are offering your gift at the altar and there remember that your brother or sister has something against you, leave your gift there in front of the altar. First go and be reconciled to them; then come and offer your gift.

Pray with thanksgiving, we can always find something to be thankful for, no matter how burdened we are by our wants or needs.

[Col 4:2 CSB] Devote yourselves to prayer; stay alert in it with thanksgiving.

Pray with persistence. We should persevere in prayer and not quit or be dejected because we have not received an immediate answer. Part of praying in GOD'S will is believing that, whether His answer is we accept His judgment, submit to GOD'S Will, and persevere in your prayers.

[Luk 18:1 NLT] One day Jesus told his disciples a story to show that they should always pray and never give up.

[1Th 5:17-18 NLT] Never stop praying. 18 Be thankful in all circumstances, for this is GOD'S will for you who belong to Christ Jesus.

The call to prayer is moving across our nation and the whole world right now because of the pandemic, the Coronavirus (COVID-19). We should pray to take away this pandemic, and we should be asking GOD to meet our needs, healing, for finances, to improve our relationships. These things we need but should not be our first focus!

Our first focus should be seeking the Kingdom of GOD. We can be confident that when we seek His Kingdom first, we are doing His will. GOD will supply us with everything else we need. This is Divine Understanding.

But when everything is going smoothly, and life is wonderful...some people forget to pray. It's foremost about asking GOD in the midst of this shaking that is underway right now to seek His Kingdom and to pray for the days ahead.

In tribulation, like what we are now seeing, we often pray to be kept safe, but not for our salvation.

[Rom 12:12 NLT] Rejoice in our confident hope. Be patient in trouble, and keep on praying.

What are you waiting for? Maybe you think you're waiting on GOD. You think you're waiting on GOD for that job. You think you're waiting on GOD for a windfall or whatever you are waiting on. Divine Understanding teaches us GOD is waiting on you. Waiting for you to plant a seed; a "seed of hope". Pray, pray for whatever.

To use a metaphor, everything in life starts as a seed: And nothing happens until the seed is planted. What does a farmer do when he's got a barren field? He doesn't complain about it. He starts planting some seed, because nothing is going to happen until he plants the seeds. The farmers field cannot produce a crop until the seeds are in the ground.

GOD cannot help you until you plant a seed. GOD will not produce what you need until your seeds are in the ground. When you have a need, don't gripe about it, don't wish about it, just pray about it — just plant a seed, a seed of hope.

Why does GOD require us to plant a seed? Because planting is an act of faith. How do you plant a seed? Through prayer! A lack of prayer demonstrates a lack of faith and a lack of trust in GOD'S Word. We pray to demonstrate our faith in GOD, that He will do as He has promised in His Word and bless our lives abundantly more than we could ask or hope for.

[Eph 3:20 NIV] Now to him who is able to do immeasurably more than all we ask or imagine, according to his power that is at work within us,

Prayer is our primary means of seeing GOD work in others' lives. Because it is our means of plugging into GOD'S power, it is our means of defeating Satan and his army that we are powerless to overcome by ourselves. Therefore, may GOD find us often before His throne, for we have a high priest in heaven who can identify with all that we go through.

[Heb 4:15-16 NIV] For we do not have a high priest who is unable to empathize with our weaknesses, but we have one who has been tempted in every way, just as we are--yet he did not sin. Let us then approach GOD'S throne of grace with confidence, so that we may receive mercy and find grace to help us in our time of need.

We have GOD'S promise that the fervent prayer of a righteous man accomplishes much (May GOD glorify His name in our lives as we believe in Him enough to come to Him often in prayer.

*[Jas 5:16 NLT] …………………….. **The earnest prayer of a righteous person has great power and produces wonderful results.***

What need have you been waiting on GOD to provide? What do you think GOD might be waiting on you to do about that need? What seed can you plant today?

Though we may struggle with believing GOD has left us fending for ourselves in hard times. His Word is filled with reminders: "seeds of hope." Our confident hope is Jesus Christ, is the son of GOD.

GOD, never said this life will be easy. He never promised that we won't get weary, or think we are not alone. Yes, there are days even the best of us believe…. He has left us alone. When everything is falling apart around us, where do you turn?

Look no further than Psalm 91 in the Bible. It gives both direction and encouragement. GOD has made some promises no one should miss here. Psalm 91 gives a word of comfort in GOD'S promises.

It calls on the readers to seek refuge in the Lord, in their troubles. It tells us we should seek comfort and protection by trusting in GOD Almighty.

It tells us GOD will protect us while we wait for His deliverance. When we live under the protection of GOD, we dwell in the shadow of the Almighty. It says GOD Himself will rescue from the destructive plague. This is a prayer everyone should say.

If you study the prayers of the Bible, you begin to notice that the prayers GOD honors and answers are those that repeat his promises back to him. Psalm 91 is one of those prayers we should repeat back to GOD. It is not just the prayers of the Bible that we should repeat back to GOD, but His words are honored as well.

Dear friend, don't underestimate this method and power of praying GOD'S Word back to Him. You can pray the Bible back to GOD when you read it. Do not just read through the Bible, pray through it! The Bible is our prayer book, so pray through it and lay hold of the promises all through the Bible. Tie the promises of GOD in the Bible to your prayer life.

[Rom 9:28 NASB] FOR THE LORD WILL EXECUTE HIS WORD ON THE EARTH, THOROUGHLY AND QUICKLY."

[Jhn 1:1 NLT] In the beginning the Word already existed. The Word was with God, and the Word was God.

Prayer can be awkward. A difficult proposition for many people and uncertainty. But Praying GOD'S Word back to Him is a simple way to pray. GOD faithfully responds to every believing prayer that is grounded upon the promises of His Word.

The Bible is a book of promises from GOD'S heart to ours. GOD does not break His word! His promises surpass anything we could pray for because each of GOD'S promises is made by the

One who possesses the authority and power to fulfill all of them perfectly.

Praying GOD'S Word is like uncovering buried treasure. Remember where your treasure is, there will be your heart. Dig up GOD'S treasure of His words and promises. GOD'S promises are a firm building block which forms the foundation for our faith.

Psa 119:160, 162 NLT] The very essence of your words is truth; all your just regulations will stand forever. ... I rejoice in your word like one who discovers a great treasure.

Whenever we pray GOD'S Word, we are put in touch with the heart of GOD. As children of GOD we have full assurance through the Holy Spirit who makes GOD'S promises a reality in our hearts. GOD'S promises are our rightful inheritance as His children. In believing and receiving His Word, we experience an incredible surge of faith in our hearts. Because our bodies are the temple of the Holy Spirit.

[Rom 8:16 NIV] The Spirit himself testifies with our spirit that we are GOD'S children.

[1Co 6:19 NIV] Do you not know that your bodies are temples of the Holy Spirit, who is in you, whom you have received from God? You are not your own;

Praying GOD'S Word back to Him, is a two-sided street. Not only must we place faith in GOD'S word, but we must also surrender our desires so that our will aligns with His. Praying GOD'S Word assures us that our requests are in accordance with GOD'S will.

If you need an example of praying GOD'S word read Matthew 6:9-13. These verses are known as the Lord's prayer. The Lord's Prayer, also called the Our Father, is a Christian prayer which Jesus taught as the way to pray.

The Lord's Prayer is important to Christians because it is what Jesus gave to his disciples as a form of prayer when they asked him to teach them how to pray. ... Pray like this. **[Mat 6:9-13 RSV] Pray then like this: Our Father who art in heaven, Hallowed be thy name. Thy kingdom come. Thy will be done, On earth as it is in heaven. Give us this day our daily bread; And forgive us our debts, As we also have forgiven our debtors; And lead us not into temptation, But deliver us from evil.**

In reciting the Lord's Prayer some will say "forgive us our debts", some will say "trespasses", and others will say "sins". This is how I learned it, (debts, debtors) but now most of the time I will say trespasses.

Jesus said, "Pray like this" meaning as an example of how to pray. These things should go into a prayer - worship, trust in God, requests, confession, protection, etc. Pray for these kinds of things, but you should speak to GOD using your own words and His. In this way you are sure to be praying in GOD'S will.

We know from (1 John 5:14-15). When our prayers are harmonious with GOD'S will, our faithful prayers resonate in heaven. As the words of GOD are spoken, our faith is reinforced. By now you understand that GOD hears all prayers of the righteous, whether silent or spoken.

The Bible shows us that the relationship between GOD the Father and the Holy Spirit is so close that the Holy Spirit's prayers on our behalf in our weakness. So our prayers need not be audible, the Holy Spirit repeats our prayers to GOD. The Holy Spirits speaks our words back to GOD.

Which inspires GOD to move on our behalf. And just think how much more GOD will move on our behalf if it is His own words that the Holy Spirit prays back to Him.

[Rom 8:26-27 NLT] And the Holy Spirit helps us in our weakness. For example, we don't know what God wants us to pray for. But the Holy Spirit prays for us with groanings that cannot be expressed in words. And the Father who knows all hearts knows what the Spirit is saying, for the Spirit pleads for us believers in harmony with GOD'S own will.

When we place GOD'S Word into personal prayers, we begin to comprehend how much God wants to enrich our lives. Praying GOD'S Word is the manifestation of His glory being lived out in our lives. We bring glory to GOD by praying His words back to Him.

I want to talk about the power of healing for just one moment. Most of us want to know; how the healing power of prayer works? Whole books have been written about the many facets of healing. But I

GOD'S Divine Understanding

want to address the command associated with healing prayer which comes from James 5:14:

[Jas 5:14-15 NLT] Are any of you sick? You should call for the elders of the church to come and pray over you, anointing you with oil in the name of the Lord. Such a prayer offered in faith will heal the sick, and the Lord will make you well. And if you have committed any sins, you will be forgiven.

GOD is a compassionate and merciful GOD, who does heal. This we know, but sometimes the healing powers seem to be in the faith of those who are praying. You can have healing if you do not go to Church. But the prayers of the elders can help, their faith is strong because of their age. And because of all the tribulation they themselves have gone through. Sometimes healing can only come from the faith of those who are praying.

Using the elders of the church is a powerful tool for healing, their faith is strong. And sometimes it is the faith of the person who is being prayed over, that brings healing. When Jesus healed a woman, He said, "Daughter, your faith has made you well". **[Mar 5:34 NLT] And he said to her, "Daughter, your faith has made you well. Go in peace. Your suffering is over."**

When Jesus healed two blind men, He said, "Because of your faith, it will happen". **[Mat 9:29 NLT] Then he touched their eyes and said, "Because of your faith, it will happen."**

And when Jairus requested healing for his daughter, Jesus said, "Don't be afraid. Just have faith, and she will be healed". **[Luk 8:50 NLT] But** *when Jesus heard what had happened, he said to Jairus, "Don't be afraid. Just have faith, and she will be healed."*

The scriptures say: By faith and the name of Jesus, we are healed. It can be the faith of the one praying over someone, or the faith of the person being prayed over. But it is Jesus name that is the consistent part of healing prayers. It is the faith that comes through Jesus that gives healing to all. Our faith in Jesus brings healing!

[Act 3:16 NIV] By faith in the name of Jesus, this man whom you see and know was made strong. It is Jesus' name and the faith that comes through him that has completely healed him, as you can all see.

Let us put it all together now.... Our faith in Jesus brings healing. The faith of others in Jesus brings healing. Praying GOD'S words bring healing when we have faith in Jesus. Praying in GOD'S will bring healing, because when we pray in GOD'S will...we have faith in Jesus Christ. We are told in every situation to take up the shield of faith.

[Eph 6:16 CSB] In every situation take up the shield of faith with which you can extinguish all the flaming arrows of the evil one.

The power of prayer should not be underestimated. The prayer of a righteous person is powerful and effective. Jesus taught, ... *"Truly I tell you, if you have faith as small as a mustard seed, you can say to this mountain, move from here to there, and it will move. Nothing will be impossible for you."*

***[Mat 17:14-16, 19-20 NIV]** When they came to the crowd, a man approached Jesus and knelt before him. "Lord, have mercy on my son," he said. "He has seizures and is suffering greatly. He often falls into the fire or into the water. I brought him to your disciples, but they could not heal him." ... Then the disciples came to Jesus in private and asked, "Why couldn't we drive it out?" He replied, "Because you have so little faith. Truly I tell you, if you have faith as small as a mustard seed, you can say to this mountain, 'Move from here to there,' and it will move. Nothing will be impossible for you."*

We briefly went over prying in the Spirit and having the Holy Spirit pray for us. But what is praying in the spirit? Praying in the Spirit is prayer with GOD'S Divine help. It is having faith in Jesus and relying on GOD to hear our prayers. Praying in the Spirit is a gift from GOD, received through our faith in Jesus Christ. It is through faith in Jesus that we receive the Holy Spirit.

***[1Co 14:1 ESV]** Pursue love, and earnestly desire the spiritual gifts, especially that you may prophesy.*

We are to pray in the Spirit on all occasions and in all kinds of prayers and requests. Praying in the spirit is letting the Holy Spirit pray for us.

***[Eph 6:18 NIV]** And pray in the Spirit on all occasions with all kinds of prayers and requests. With this in mind, be alert and always keep on praying for all the Lord's people.*

The Spirit helps us in our weakness. We do not know what we ought to pray for, but the Holy

Spirit himself intercedes for us, through wordless groans. And the Holy Spirit searches our hearts knowing the mind of our Spirit. Because the Holy Spirit intercedes for believers, He is always doing the will of GOD in us. We know our prayers said by the Holy Spirit is in accordance with the will of GOD.

[Rom 8:26 NLT] And the Holy Spirit helps us in our weakness. For example, we don't know what God wants us to pray for. But the Holy Spirit prays for us with groanings that cannot be expressed in words.

Now follow this, I call it a 'two-fer"! Ask the Holy Spirit to pray for you. By praying GOD'S words back to Him, Romans 8.26.

"Holy Spirit please pray for me in my weakness. I do not know what to pray for, or what to say to GOD. Please pray for me in groanings that cannot be expressed in words". In Jesus name I pray Amen. (John Spiker). May, 2020

When we pray, the two-fer- we are praying in the Spirit and praying GOD'S words back to Him at the same time. And we know this kind of prayer is in accordance with GOD'S will. Maybe I should call it the three-fer. (There will be more examples of praying GOD'S Words back to Him, at the end of this chapter.)

There is even a way to pray GOD'S Words back to Him against the Coronavirus: Ask the Holy Spirit to pray for you. By praying GOD'S words back to Him from Psalm 91.

"Holy Spirit please pray for me in my weakness. I call upon you Lord concerning my

refuge and rescue form the Coronavirus plague. You are my fortress and it is in you I trust. You yourself can rescue me from all traps and from the destructive plague. I will fear no plague or pestilence that stalks at night or the day. Under your wings I will take refuge, your faithfulness will be a protective shield". Thank You GOD. In Jesus name I pray Amen. (John Spiker) May 2020

One part then of what it means to pray in the Spirit is to pray with the help of the Holy Spirit. The Holy Spirit is constantly reminding us of our position as children of GOD. And as such, we can pray to GOD and have the Holy Spirit pray on our behalf equal the same.

What is praying in tongues, is it praying in the spirit?

Is Spirit the same as the Holy Spirit? It is helpful to acknowledge that there are varying degrees of what the Spirit is. And that there are varying degrees of experiencing the Holy Spirit in Prayer. Admittedly, opinions vary about the exact meaning of praying in the Spirit. And there are many different claims on how to achieve prayer in the Spirit. I am positive about one thing- it is not a skill to be acquired. It is a gift from GOD.

There are a lot of people teaching that praying in the Spirit is synonymous with praying in tongues. Praying in tongues is a gift of the Spirit but is not the same as praying in the Spirit. It is the fruit of the Spirit. Understand, not all Christians can speak in tongues. So when the Bible tells us to pray in the Spirit on all occasions; we can know that praying in tongues is distinct from praying in the Spirit.

1 Corinthians 12- speaks on spiritual gifts. These extraordinary spiritual gifts are the word of wisdom, the word of knowledge, increased faith, the gifts of healing, the gift of miracles, prophecy, the discernment of spirits, diverse kinds of tongues (speaking in tongues) and interpretation of tongues.

The Gifts of the Holy Spirit are unique skills and abilities given by the Holy Spirit to faithful followers of Christ to serve GOD for the common good of the church. GOD empowers the faithful with Spiritual gifts to do what they are called to do. 2Peter 1:3 says, GOD has given us everything we need for life. The gifts of the Holy Spirit are part of everything we need to live a godly life.

[2Pe 1:3 NLT] By his divine power, God has given us everything we need for living a godly life. We have received all of this by coming to know him, the one who called us to himself by means of his marvelous glory and excellence.

The Bible says, we have different gifts, given to us according to the grace of GOD. And that we are to use them in proportion to our faith.

[Rom 12:6-8 NIV] We have different gifts, according to the grace given to each of us. If your gift is prophesying, then prophesy in accordance with your faith; if it is serving, then serve; if it is teaching, then teach; if it is to encourage, then give encouragement; if it is giving, then give generously; if it is to lead, do it diligently; if it is to show mercy, do it cheerfully.

How do you know if you have received the gift to pray in the Spirit? How do you know if you are experiencing the Holy Spirit? How can you acquire the Holy Spirit? How do you know if the Holy Spirit is talking to you? What is the evidence that the Holy Spirit is working in you? All are good questions?

You receive the gift to pray in the Spirit, by believing in GOD. Praying in the Spirit is prayer with divine help. It's trusting in faith and relying on GOD to hear, understand, and act.

[Jde 1:20 NKJV] But you, beloved, building yourselves up on your most holy faith, praying in the Holy Spirit,

There are assorted theological claims about how to achieve praying in the Spirit as if it is a skill that can be acquired. Like praying in tongues. It is not. Praying in the Spirit is a gift we receive because of our faith in Jesus Christ, the gift of the Holy Spirit. We can pray in the Spirit because of the Holy Spirit, in spite-of praying in tongues.

[Act 2:38 CSB] Peter replied, "Repent and be baptized, each of you, in the name of Jesus Christ for the forgiveness of your sins, and you will receive the gift of the Holy Spirit.

[1Co 12:4, NIV] There are different kinds of gifts, but the same Spirit distributes them. ...

There are different Spiritual gifts and they all come from the Holy Spirit. Remember that believers received the Holy Spirit on the day of Pentecost. And since that day, all believers receive the Holy Spirit. We learned about the Day of Pentecost in chapter 3.

Is the Power of Praying in the Spirit... speaking in tongues? Many and I say many theological experts say praying in the spirit is speaking in tongues. Wrong! I will tell you these people are a lot smarter than I will ever be. But this does not mean they cannot be wrong. Hear me out first, yes, speaking in tongues is a spiritual gift.

And yes, the Holy Spirit prays in tongue. The Holy Spirit understands all tongues. So to these people who say praying in the Spirit is praying in tongues. this is right! Yes, they are right to an extent. Praying in the spirit can be speaking in tongues, but praying in tongues is a gift, and is not given to all believers. Whereas, praying in the Spirit is for all who believe. Understand, praying in tongues is not the only way to pray in the Spirit.

Therefore, where I have a problem is when these people say that praying in the spirit is speaking in tongues and that is all it is, there is no other way to pray in the spirit..then tongues.

[1Co 14:14-15 CSB] *For if I pray in another tongue, my spirit prays, but my understanding is unfruitful. What then? I will pray with the spirit, and I will also pray with my understanding. I will sing praise with the spirit, and I will also sing praise with my understanding.*

Praying in tongues, is unless and unfruitful, if no one can understand it. But no prayer by anyone is ever unless or unfruitful if prayer in GOD'S will.

Do you see the scripture above where it says: *"What then? I will pray with the spirit, and I will also pray with my understanding....".* Praying with the Spirit is praying with both, tongue, and understanding. Understand that the Holy Spirit helps us in our weakness, the Holy Spirit prays for us in harmony with GOD'S Will.

[Rom 8:26-27 NLT] And the Holy Spirit helps us in our weakness. For example, we don't know what God wants us to pray for. But the Holy Spirit prays for us with groanings that cannot be expressed in words. And the Father who knows all hearts knows what the Spirit is saying, for the Spirit pleads for us believers in harmony with God's own will.

However, many people misunderstand the purpose of the gift of tongues and the scriptures that describe it. At one time, I did believe that speaking in tongues was praying in the Spirit. If I wanted to pray in the spirit I had to speak in tongues. I believed that there was no other way to speak through the spirt then tongues.

But some Bible verse caused me to question my position. Understand, speaking in tongues is a gift from GOD. So if I did not have the gift, then I would not be able to pray in the spirit. The Bible makes it clear on what kind of gift tongues are; it is intended as a sign for unbelievers. And is not given to all believers, like the Holy Spirit.

[1Co 14:22-23 CSB] Speaking in other tongues, then, is intended as a sign, not for believers but for unbelievers, while prophecy is not for unbelievers but for believers. If, therefore, the whole church assembles together and all are speaking in other tongues and

people who are outsiders or unbelievers come in, will they not say that you are out of your minds?

Understand the gift of the Holy Spirit is given to all believers, not just a few. Speaking in tongues is a gift given to some, not all. Prayer in the spirit is for all. All believers can pray in the Spirit. Understand speaking in tongues is a sign for unbelievers.

Whereas, Prayer in the Spirit is for believers. Anyone who speaks in tongues edifies themselves and not the common good.

[1Co 12:7 NIV] Now to each one the manifestation of the Spirit is given for the common good.

[1Co 14:4 NIV] Anyone who speaks in a tongue edifies themselves, but the one who prophesies edifies the church.

Conclusion: Praying in tongues is speaking and praying in the Spirit. In fact, we know that the Holy Spirit does pray in tongues...Romans, says, the Holy Spirit helps us in our weakness praying with groanings that cannot be expressed in words. The Holy Spirit himself intercedes for us, through wordless groans.

But praying in tongues is not the only way to pray in the Spirit. Praying in tongues is a gift from the Holy Spirit and a sign for unbelievers. Everyone does not receive the gift of praying in tongues, but all believers receive the Holy Spirit. Anyone who speaks in tongues edifies themselves and not the common good. The Holy Spirit is for the common good.

Praying in the Spirit is for all, in fact we are told to pray in the Spirit. We read in Ephesians 6- where we are told to pray at all times in the Spirit. This would be impossible if the only way to pray in the Spirit was through tongues. Only a few could pray like that.

Praying in the Spirit is a gift from GOD, received through our faith in Jesus Christ. It is through faith in Jesus that we receive the Holy Spirit, which lets us pray in the Spirit. So praying in the Spirit is praying through the Holy Spirit.

I invite you to read and speak GOD'S word to be renewed by the Holy Spirit. And you should invite the Holy Spirit to pray for you. So you can find GOD'S, *"pleasing and perfect will."*

Be transformed by renewing of your mind. Love, Joy, and Patience are all products of The Fruit of the Holy Spirit. I do believe that all Christians desire to exhibit these qualities in their lives. To live as Jesus Christ did.

[1Ti 2:1-5 NLT] I urge you, first of all, to pray for all people. Ask God to help them; intercede on their behalf, and give thanks for them. Pray this way for kings and all who are in authority so that we can live peaceful and quiet lives marked by godliness and dignity. This is good and pleases God our Savior, who wants everyone to be saved and to understand the truth. For there is only one God and one Mediator who can reconcile God and humanity--the man Christ Jesus.

- **Fasting, what is it and how can it help with our prayers?**

Fasting is abstaining from food or drink in order to focus on prayer and seeking GOD Will. Fasting is essentially giving up something, not always food, for a period of time in order to focus your thoughts on God. Fasting does come in a variety of forms.

I would be remiss if I didn't say something about the variety of ways in which one might fast. Contrary to what many think, one need not always fast from food or drink to achieve the desired goal. You can give up anything that will allow you to focus on GOD. You may choose to fast from caffeine or soda or liquids that you regularly consume. Or fast from a TV show, or some sport.

You may choose to fast from sugar or from some sort of food that is a regular part of your diet. Perhaps you choose only to eat fruits or vegetables for the length of the fast, refraining from all meat (or vice versa). In the case of both of the former two forms of fasting, you would continue to eat and drink other items to maintain your strength and health. There is an endless supply of things you can fast from. But before you do, make sure you dedicate it GOD.

Spend the time praying that you would have used for whatever you chose to give up. There are degrees of fasting. There is a regular fast which consists of abstaining from all food and drink except for water. A partial fast is when one abstains from some particular kind of food or activity.

You may also wish to fast from all food for only a particular meal each day. In other words, you may choose to skip lunch for a day or two or a week, or dinner, or even breakfast. All such forms of partial fasting are entirely appropriate. As long as you dedicate it GOD.

Say something like; Heaven Father I wish to fast from_____. I dedicate this fast to you, and your Son Jesus, and seek your help in_____. OH, Holy Spirit please guide me in my Fast, Amen. In Jesus name I pray.

A complete or absolute fast that entails no food or liquid of any kind, should only be for a very short period of time. Always seek medical advice before any kind of food or liquid fast.

If you have unique physical problems that would make fasting dangerous or unhealthy, please do not alter your prescribed regimen of medication or of eating and drinking without first consulting with your physician.

There is nothing to be ashamed of if you cannot fast in regard to food and drink. Simply choose another way to fast. How long you fast is entirely up to you. But you should ask the Holy Spirit on how to fast and how long to fast.

Both the Old Testament and New Testament teach the value of fasting. Scripture tells us that fasting will help us grow a more intimate relationship with Christ and will open our eyes to what He wants to teach us.

There are many examples of people in the Bible who fasted, we see how GOD grants supernatural revelation and wisdom through this practice. While fasting, many people read the Bible, pray, or worship. Fasting is often a way of expressing grief or a means of humbling one's self before the Lord.

Here are a few things fasting and pray can do:

1. Fasting and prayer can help us hear from GOD.

2. Fasting and prayer can reveal our hidden sin.

3. Fasting and prayer can strengthen intimacy with GOD.

4. Fasting and prayer can teach us to pray with the right motives.

5. Fasting and prayer can build our faith.

6. It enables the Holy Spirit to reveal your true spiritual condition, resulting in brokenness, repentance, and a transformed life.

When we fast and pray, we are taking time away from a meal or an activity to devote our entire being to focus on God. We find we are more sensitive to the voice of GOD, more attuned to hearing what He has to reveal to us. Fasting is a biblical way to truly humble yourself in the sight of GOD.

I have read somewhere where someone said that Jesus disciples did not fast. And they say read Matthew 9:14, where John's disciples asked Jesus, "Why do we and the Pharisees fast often, but your disciples do not fast? But now read what Jesus said. He said, they will fast when He will be taken away. You see this person did not give Jesus answered.

[Mat 9:14-15 CSB] Then John's disciples came to him, saying, "Why do we and the Pharisees fast often, but your disciples do not fast?" Jesus said to them, "Can the wedding guests be sad while the groom is with them? The time will come when the groom will be taken away from them, and then they will fast.

In Matthew 6:16, Jesus words imply that fasting was a regular practice in His follower's lives. When teaching His disciples basic principles of godly living and speaking on fasting, He begins with, "When you fast," not "If you fast." So we understand fasting was an everyday part of the lives of Jesus disciples.

[Mat 6:16-18 NLT] "And when you fast, don't make it obvious, as the hypocrites do, for they try to look miserable and disheveled so people will admire them for their fasting. I tell you the truth, that is the only reward they will ever get. But when you fast, comb your hair and wash your face. Then no one will notice that you are fasting, except your Father, who knows what you do in private. And your Father, who sees everything, will reward you.

After being baptized by John the Baptist, Jesus was tempted by the devil for 40 days and nights in the Judaean Desert. It was at this time that Jesus had fasted forty days and forty nights.

During this time, Satan came to Jesus and tried to tempt him. Jesus having refused each temptation, Satan then departed, and Jesus returned to Galilee to begin His ministry. Jesus did not begin His ministry until He had fasted.

[Mat 4:1-2 CSB] Then Jesus was led up by the Spirit into the wilderness to be tempted by the devil. After he had fasted forty days and forty nights, he was hungry.

We see in Mark 9 17 the story where the disciples of Jesus couldn't heal a boy by casting out an evil spirit. So the father of the boy brought the boy to Jesus. The father asked Jesus to have mercy on us and help if he could.

"What do you mean, 'If I can'?" Jesus asked. "Anything is possible if a person believes." The father instantly cried out, "I do believe, but help me overcome my unbelief!" Jesus rebuked the evil spirit, it left him. Afterward, when Jesus was alone in the house with his disciples, they asked him, "Why couldn't we cast out that evil spirit?"

Jesus said: ***[Mar 9:29 HNV] He said to them, "This kind can come out by nothing, except by prayer and fasting."***

So some things can only be accomplished by prayer and fasting. Although the Bible does not give a direct command on this issue, examples of fasting appear in both the Old and the New Testaments. There are more verses in the Bible about fasting. Here are just a few:

Part day fast: ***[Jdg 20:26 NLT] Then all the Israelites went up to Bethel and wept in the presence of the LORD and fasted until evening. ...***

All day fast: ***[1Sa 7:6 NLT] ……..They also went without food all day and confessed that they had sinned against the LORD.***

Group fasting and to repent: **[Neh 9:1 NLT] On October 31 the people assembled again, and this time they fasted and dressed in burlap and sprinkled dust on their heads.**

To show grief. Nehemiah mourned, fasted, and prayed when he learned Jerusalem's walls had been broken down. **[Neh 1:4 CSB] When I heard these words, I sat down and wept. I mourned for a number of days, fasting and praying before the God of the heavens.**

All night fast: **[Dan 6:18 NASB] Then the king went off to his palace and spent the night fasting, and no entertainment was brought before him; and his sleep fled from him.**

A three-day fast: **[Est 4:16 NASB] "Go, assemble all the Jews who are found in Susa, and fast for me; do not eat or drink for three days, night or day........**

A seven-day fast: **[1Sa 31:13 NASB] They took their bones and buried them under the tamarisk tree at Jabesh, and fasted seven days.**

A fourteen-day fast: **[Act 27:33 NASB] Until the day was about to dawn, Paul was encouraging them all to take some food, saying, "Today is the fourteenth day that you have been constantly watching and going without eating, having taken nothing.**

A twenty-one day fast: **[Dan 10:3 NIV] ate no choice food; no meat or wine touched my lips; and I used no lotions at all until the three weeks were over.**

A fast of unspecified lengths, and show that the Holy Spirit talk to them while they were worshiping and fasting: **[Act 13:2 NIV] While they were worshiping the Lord and fasting, the Holy Spirit said, "Set apart for me Barnabas and Saul for the work to which I have called them."**

The disciples fasted while making decisions. To seek GOD'S wisdom. Paul and Barnabas prayed and fasted for the elders of the churches before committing them to the Lord for His service. **[Act 14:23 NIV] Paul and Barnabas appointed elders for them in each church and, with prayer and fasting, committed them to the Lord,**

To seek deliverance or protection. Ezra declared a fast and prayed for a safe journey for the Israelites. **[Ezr 8:21 CSB] I proclaimed a fast by the Ahava River, so that we might humble ourselves before our God and ask him for a safe journey for us, our dependents, and all our possessions.**

To gain victory. After losing 40,000 men in battle in two days, the Israelites cried out to God for help. The next day the Lord gave them victory over the Benjamites. **[Jdg 20:26 CSB] 2The whole Israelite army went to Bethel where they wept and sat before the LORD. They fasted that day until evening and offered burnt offerings and fellowship offerings to the LORD.**

We see in Joel 2:12 where the Lord says, "Turn to me now, while there is time. Give me your hearts. Come with fasting, weeping, and mourning. **[Joe 2:12 NLT] That is why the LORD says, "Turn to me now, while there is time. Give me** *your hearts. Come with fasting, weeping, and mourning.*

There is great power in prayer GOD'S Word back to Him, and even more power when it is combined when fasting. I do believe when the two are combined, something supernatural from GOD gets released to accomplish His Word. GOD'S word always produces fruit.

[Isa 55:11 NLT] It is the same with my word. I send it out, and it always produces fruit. It will accomplish all I want it to, and it will prosper everywhere I send it.

John Spiker,

Chapter 6
Seeds of Hope

[Mat 6:27, 31-34 NLT] Can all your worries add a single moment to your life? ... "So don't worry about these things, saying, 'What will we eat? What will we drink? What will we wear?' These things dominate the thoughts of unbelievers, but your heavenly Father already knows all your needs. Seek the Kingdom of God above all else, and live righteously, and he will give you everything you need. "So don't worry about tomorrow, for tomorrow will bring its own worries. Today's trouble is enough for today.

It is easy to feel hopeless, these days in our times of trouble. We all feel hopeless in times of emotional or physical hardship. But the Bible teaches us, "with God all things are possible." Call on these prayers when you (or a loved one) are struggling through everyday life-altering challenges. Dear Lord Jesus you've told us to come to you and ask for our every need in life as it is written in scripture:

• It says in Scripture you do listen and pay attention to our prayers, this I have confidence in. GOD, I believe in the power of prayer, and wait to hear from you. In Jesus name I pray Amen. (John Spiker) May 2020

• I pray to you O GOD, to be always full of joy in every situation. Let me rejoice in Jesus Christ coming soon and worry about nothing. Instead let me remember to pray about everything. You know all I need LORD, and I thank you for all you have done, and will do in my life. In Jesus name I pray Amen. (John Spiker) May 2020

• Loving God, I pray that you will comfort me in my suffering, As I struggle through the trials of everyday life. Please lend skill to the hands of my healers, and bless the means used for my cure. Give me such confidence in the power of your grace, that even when I am afraid, I may put my whole trust in you; with you God all things are possible through our Savior Jesus Christ we pray, Amen (John Spiker) May 2020

• Lamb of God, who takes away the sins of the world, send us Thy Holy Spirit. Lamb of God, who takes away the sins of the world, pour down into our souls the gifts of the Holy Spirit. Lamb of God, who takes away the sins of the world, grant us the Spirit of wisdom and health in mind and body. Come, Holy Spirit! Fill the hearts of Thy faithful and

kindle in us the fire of Thy love. Amen. Taken from many prayers to the Lamb of GOD and prayers to the Holy Spirit.(John Spiker)

Prayer to the Holy Spirit can be a wonderful source of reflection. Made up from prayers to the Holy Spirit.

- *Come, Holy Spirit, pour into us, all your spiritual gifts. Send forth your Spirit and make us into a new creation. O Holy Spirit you are the Spirit Jesus promised to send, so please come to us. You transformed the first disciples, transform us into the person GOD wants us to be. Enlightening our minds and hearts. Help us listen for GOD and understand Him in all our ways. Holy Spirit bless us with great joy and the peace of GOD. Bless us with courage to live each day for GOD, and to be truly wise. Teach us to ever rejoice in the Lord. And bless us with health all the days of our lives. Amen. (John Spiker) May 2020*

[Psa 35:27 NLT] ."Great is the LORD, who delights in blessing his servant with peace!"

[Eph 3:12 NLT] Because of Christ and our faith in him, we can now come boldly and confidently into God's presence.

[Psa 143:1 CSB] LORD, hear my prayer. In your faithfulness listen to my plea, and in your righteousness answer me

Start all prayers with the "our Father" Then say Psalm 4:1.

**Our Father, who art in heaven,
hallowed be thy name;
thy kingdom come;
thy will be done on earth as it is in heaven.**

*Give us this day our daily bread;
and forgive us our trespasses as we
forgive those who trespass against us;
and lead us not into temptation,
but deliver us from evil.*

For thine is the kingdom and the power and the glory now and forever. Amen.

[Psa 4:1 NLT] Answer me when I call to you, O God who declares me innocent. Free me from my troubles. Have mercy on me and hear my prayer. Amen.

God is known by many names in the Bible. Each name reveals a certain aspect of His character: Jehovah-Rapha, in Hebrew, is one such name and found in the Old Testament and means "The God who heals" (Exodus 15:26) El Roi, in Hebrew, another name found in the Old Testament and means "The God who see me" (Genesis 16:13) And Jesus himself said, "Righteous Father". (John 17:25). And "Father in Heaven". (Matthew 5:16)

Lets us Pray

"Our Father in heaven, Hallowed be thy names": Jehovah-Rapha, the God who heals: And El Ro, the God who sees me... Righteous Father, I come humbly before you this day and seek your peace and rest, for myself and my family, in every area of our lives, as it is written. Father, we know that you can heal us in a heartbeat. We pray for Your miraculous healing today: From depression, and all disease.

We pray for miraculous healing because we know you are as capable of fixing our physicalities as you are to hold the universe in your hands. Father, through Your Son's death on the cross, we have the opportunity to be Saved and come before you.

And by Prayer we have the opportunity to be healed in body and soul. By believing in Jesus we are able to connect straight to You in prayer. Bless our hearts to believe in You beyond our heart's capacity. Strengthen our faith where it is weak and strengthen our resolve to linger in Your presence a little longer each and every day.

Please forgive us our sins, cleanse us of all unrighteousness, and begin your healing from the inside out. Lord, we give you all our hurt, pain, weakness and sorrow in exchange for your comfort, love and peace.

Blessed Holy Trinity, Father, Son and Holy Spirit, we thank you for the many blessings my family and I receive each and every day. We pray you may bless and fill us with love, peace and prosperity. We also pray for an abundance of joy and the strength to live each day for you.

We pray for great health, continued healing, and your peace and salvation. We pray for your kindness and mercy. We pray for your guidance and protection. Please show us the right choices to make so that we can glorify you each day!

Bless our days and nights with prosperity for our good and for your glory. May the love of the Father, the tenderness of the Son, and the presence of the Holy Spirit, gladden our hearts and bring peace to our souls, today and for all the days of our lives. Dear God, make our day's useful, our nights restful and our efforts fruitful.

We are ever grateful to you for the prosperity and peace you have so abundantly bestowed upon us. We place our faith and trust in you. And ask that you uplift any and all obstacles that are preventing further prosperity and peace of mind in our lives. We humbly ask you for healing from all sickness and disease. Please bring us true and total health and happiness.

Please remove any snares of evil, or other negative forces working against us, our business, our family, and friends. We place our burdens in your hands, knowing that it is through your mercy that we can prosper and receive health. These things we ask in Jesus Christ's name, our Lord. Amen. John R. Spiker 02/20/20.

GOD'S words taken from, Romans 15:13. Pray these words back to GOD in confidence that He will hear your prayer.

- I pray to you GOD, the source of all hope to completely fill me with joy and pace because I trust in you. Let me overflow with confident hope through the power of the Holy Spirit. Amen. In Jesus name I pray Amen. (John Spiker) May 2020
- Praying GOD'S Words back to Him from; Jeremiah 33.
- *Lord you will certainly bring health and healing to me and you will indeed heal me. You will let me experience the abundance of true*

peace. You will restore my health and purify me from all my iniquities I committed against you.

You will rebuild me to my former health. My body will rejoice with joy, praise, and glory before all people, for the Glory of your name. People everywhere will hear of the miracle of healing you have given me. They will be amazed with awe because of all the good, peace, and prosperity you have blessed me with. Thank You GOD. In Jesus name I pray Amen. (John Spiker) May 2020

Praying GOD'S Words back to Him from; 2Corinthians 1:1

- *Father GOD and Lord Jesus Christ, please grant me your Peace and Grace. All praise to you, you are a merciful Father the source of all comfort. Please comfort us in all our troubles so that we can comfort others in their troubles. We know that even when we are weighed down with troubles it is your peace that brings us Salvation. Thank You GOD. In Jesus name I pray Amen. (John Spiker) May 2020*

This prayer was made up through many of GOD'S Words in the Bible: You can confidently say this prayer knowing you are speaking GOD'S Words back to HIM:

- *LORD GOD you are gracious and compassionate, slow to anger, abounding in faithful love. LORD come to me and leave a blessing behind. Have pity on me O LORD. Rescue me from all illness and disease and sadness. Protect my life from all evil.*

LORD you say, do not be anxious about anything, but in every situation, by pray, fasting and petition, present our request to you with thanksgiving. By doing so, you promise you will listen to our plea. So I thank you Father for hearing my prayer.

Hear my prayer O LORD, listen to my plea. Answer me because you are faithful and righteous. Do not put your servant on trial, for no one is innocent before you.

How long, O LORD, will you look on and do nothing? O LORD, you know all about my troubles. Please do not stay silent any longer. Let everyone see that you are considerate and merciful in all that you do.

LORD, hear my prayer; let my cry for help come before you. Do not hide your face from me in my time of trouble. Listen closely to me; answer me quickly when I call.

LORD my GOD, I remember the days of old. I ponder all your great works and think about what you have done and give all thanks to you. I lift my hands to you in prayer. I thirst for you as parched land thirsts for rain. Bend down and listen to your servant and answer me when I call for help.

Come quickly, LORD, and answer me. Do not abandon me now, O LORD. Wake up! Rise to my defense! Take up my case, my GOD and my LORD. Declare me not guilty of my sins and heal me of all my disease and illness.

O LORD my GOD for you give justice and are considerate and merciful. Show your unfailing love to me, for I am trusting in Your mercy. Show me where to walk and teach me to do your will for you are my GOD.

May your gracious Holy Spirit lead me forward on a firm footing. For the glory of your name, O LORD, preserve my life. Because of your faithfulness, bring me out of this distress. In your unfailing love heal me and silence all my enemies and destroy all my foes, for I am your servant. In Jesus name I pray Amen. (John Spiker) May 2020

This prayer was made up through many of GOD'S Words in the Bible: You can confidently say this prayer knowing you are speaking GOD'S Words back to HIM:

- *LORD, it is written in Scripture, that we are to cast our cares on you, and you will sustain us. Please LORD for your word, hear my plea. YOU word says you will never let the righteous be shaken. Therefore, since we have been made right in Your sight by faith. Send us your peace and blessings.*

It is because of our faith in Jesus Christ that we were brought into the place of undeserved privilege where we now stand, and we confidently and joyfully look forward to our healing and sharing of your GLORY. We can rejoice, too, when we run into problems and trials, for we know you are always there to help. In Jesus name I pray Amen. (John Spiker) May 2020

Let me experience your peace, which exceeds anything I can imagine or understand. O LORD I ask you to guard my heart, mind and protect me from all evil. Please let the Holy Spirit live in me, as I try to live in Jesus Christ. In Jesus name I pray Amen. (John Spiker) May 2020

• *Heal me, LORD, and I will be healed; save me, and I will be saved, for you are my GOD. The LORD has heard my plea; the LORD will answer my prayer. Amen. In Jesus name I pray Amen. (John Spiker) May 2020*

Prayers right from the Bible. Pray as is or change the words to pray back to GOD.

[Jer 17:14 NLT] O LORD, if you heal me, I will be truly healed; if you save me, I will be truly saved. My praises are for you alone!

[Phl 4:4-7 NLT] Always be full of joy in the Lord. I say it again--rejoice! Let everyone see that you are considerate in all you do. Remember, the Lord is coming soon. Don't worry about anything; instead, pray about everything. Tell God what you need and thank him for all he has done. Then you will experience God's peace, which exceeds anything we can understand. His peace will guard your hearts and minds as you live in Christ Jesus.

[Mic 7:7 CSB] 7 But I will look to the LORD; I will wait for the God of my salvation. My God will hear me.

[1Jo 5:14-15 CSB] This is the confidence we have before him: If we ask anything according to his will, he hears us. And if we know that he hears whatever we ask, we know that we have what we have asked of him.

[Eph 3:14-21 CSB] For this reason I kneel before the Father from whom every family in heaven and on earth is named. I pray that he may grant you, according to the riches of his glory, to be strengthened with power in your inner being through his Spirit, and that Christ may dwell in your hearts through faith. I pray that you, being rooted and firmly established in love, may be able to comprehend with all the saints what is the length and width, height and depth of God's love, and to know Christ's love that surpasses knowledge, so that you may be filled with all the fullness of God. Now to him who is able to do above and beyond all that we ask or think according to the power that works in us -- to him be glory in the church and in Christ Jesus to all generations, forever and ever. Amen.

Prayers of Worship:

[Psa 99:1-9 CSB] The LORD reigns! Let the peoples tremble. He is enthroned between the cherubim. Let the earth quake. The LORD is great in Zion; he is exalted above all the peoples. Let them praise your great and awe-inspiring name. He is holy. The mighty King loves justice. You have established fairness; you have administered justice and righteousness in Jacob. Exalt the LORD our God; bow in worship at his footstool. He is holy. Moses and Aaron were among his priests; Samuel also was among those calling on his name. They called to the LORD and he answered them. He spoke to them in a pillar of cloud; they

kept his decrees and the statutes he gave them. LORD our God, you answered them. You were a forgiving God to them, but an avenger of their sinful actions. Exalt the LORD our God; bow in worship at his holy mountain, for the LORD our God is holy.

[Psa 103:1-22 NLT] A psalm of David. Let all that I am praise the LORD; with my whole heart, I will praise his holy name. Let all that I am praise the LORD; may I never forget the good things he does for me. He forgives all my sins and heals all my diseases. He redeems me from death and crowns me with love and tender mercies. He fills my life with good things. My youth is renewed like the eagle's! The LORD gives righteousness and justice to all who are treated unfairly. He revealed his character to Moses and his deeds to the people of Israel. The LORD is compassionate and merciful, slow to get angry and filled with unfailing love. He will not constantly accuse us, nor remain angry forever. He does not punish us for all our sins; he does not deal harshly with us, as we deserve. For his unfailing love toward those who fear him is as great as the height of the heavens above the earth. He has removed our sins as far from us as the east is from the west. The LORD is like a father to his children, tender and compassionate to those who fear him. For he knows how weak we are; he remembers we are only dust. Our days on earth are like grass; like wildflowers, we bloom and die. The wind blows,

and we are gone--as though we had never been here. But the love of the LORD remains forever with those who fear him. His salvation extends to the children's children of those who are faithful to his covenant, of those who obey his commandments! The LORD has made the heavens his throne; from there he rules over everything. Praise the LORD, you angels, you mighty ones who carry out his plans, listening for each of his commands. Yes, praise the LORD, you armies of angels who serve him and do his will! Praise the LORD, everything he has created, everything in all his kingdom. Let all that I am praise the LORD.

[Psa 69:30, 34 NLT] 30 Then I will praise God's name with singing, and I will honor him with thanksgiving. ... 34 Praise him, O heaven and earth, the seas and all that move in them.

Prayers of Faith:

[Heb 11:1 NLT] 1 Faith is the confidence that what we hope for will actually happen; it gives us assurance about things we cannot see.

[Rom 3:21-26 NLT] But now God has shown us a way to be made right with him without keeping the requirements of the law, as was promised in the writings of Moses and the prophets long ago. We are made right with God by placing our faith in Jesus Christ. And this is true for everyone who believes, no matter who we are. For everyone has sinned; we all fall short of God's glorious standard. Yet God, with undeserved kindness, declares that we are righteous. He did this through Christ Jesus

when he freed us from the penalty for our sins. For God presented Jesus as the sacrifice for sin. People are made right with God when they believe that Jesus sacrificed his life, shedding his blood. This sacrifice shows that God was being fair when he held back and did not punish those who sinned in times past, for he was looking ahead and including them in what he would do in this present time. God did this to demonstrate his righteousness, for he himself is fair and just, and he declares sinners to be right in his sight when they believe in Jesus.

[Psa 91:1-16 NLT] Those who live in the shelter of the Most High will find rest in the shadow of the Almighty. This I declare about the LORD: He alone is my refuge, my place of safety; he is my God, and I trust him. For he will rescue you from every trap and protect you from deadly disease. He will cover you with his feathers. He will shelter you with his wings. His faithful promises are your armor and protection. Do not be afraid of the terrors of the night, nor the arrow that flies in the day. Do not dread the disease that stalks in darkness, nor the disaster that strikes at midday. Though a thousand fall at your side, though ten thousand are dying around you, these evils will not touch you. Just open your eyes, and see how the wicked are punished. If you make the LORD your refuge, if you make the Most High your shelter, no evil will conquer you; no plague will come near your home. For he will order his angels to protect you

wherever you go. They will hold you up with their hands so you won't even hurt your foot on a stone. You will trample upon lions and cobras; you will crush fierce lions and serpents under your feet! The LORD says, "I will rescue those who love me. I will protect those who trust in my name. When they call on me, I will answer; I will be with them in trouble. I will rescue and honor them. I will reward them with a long life and give them my salvation."

[1Ki 8:28 NLT] 28 Nevertheless, listen to my prayer and my plea, O LORD my God. Hear the cry and the prayer that your servant is making to you today.

[Neh 1:5-6 NLT] 5 Then I said, "O LORD, God of heaven, the great and awesome God who keeps his covenant of unfailing love with those who love him and obey his commands, 6 listen to my prayer! Look down and see me praying night and day for your people Israel. I confess that we have sinned against you. Yes, even my own family and I have sinned!

[Psa 6:1-9 NLT] 1 A psalm of David, O LORD, don't rebuke me in your anger or discipline me in your rage. Have compassion on me, LORD, for I am weak. Heal me, LORD, for my bones are in agony. I am sick at heart. How long, O LORD, until you restore me? Return, O LORD, and rescue me. Save me because of your unfailing love. For the dead do not remember you. Who can praise you from the grave? I am worn out from sobbing. All night I flood my bed with weeping, drenching it with my tears. My

vision is blurred by grief; my eyes are worn out because of all my enemies. Go away, all you who do evil, for the LORD has heard my weeping. The LORD has heard my plea; the LORD will answer my prayer.

[Psa 54:-2 NLT] Come with great power, O God, and rescue me! Defend me with your might. 2 Listen to my prayer, O God. Pay attention to my plea.

[Psa 55:1-2 NLT] Listen to my prayer, O God. Do not ignore my cry for help! 2 Please listen and answer me, for I am overwhelmed by my troubles.

[Psa 69:13, 16-17, 29 NLT] 13 But I keep praying to you, LORD, hoping this time you will show me favor. In your unfailing love, O God, answer my prayer with your sure salvation. ... Answer my prayers, O LORD, for your unfailing love is wonderful. Take care of me, for your mercy is so plentiful. Don't hide from your servant; answer me quickly, for I am in deep trouble! ... I am suffering and in pain. Rescue me, O God, by your saving power.

Made Right with GOD:

[Rom 3:28-31 NLT] So we are made right with God through faith and not by obeying the law. After all, is God the God of the Jews only? Isn't he also the God of the Gentiles? Of course he is. There is only one God, and he makes people right with himself only by faith, whether they are Jews or Gentiles. Well then, if we emphasize faith, does this mean that we can

forget about the law? Of course not! In fact, only when we have faith do we truly fulfill the law.

[Psa 118:21 NLT] I thank you for answering my prayer and giving me victory!

[Psa 5:11-12 CSB] But let all who take refuge in you rejoice; let them shout for joy forever. May you shelter them and may those who love your name boast about you. For you, LORD, bless the righteous one; you surround him with favor like a shield.

[Rom 5:1-5 CSB] Therefore, since we have been declared righteous by faith, we have peace with God through our Lord Jesus Christ. We have also obtained access through him by faith into this grace in which we stand, and we rejoice in the hope of the glory of God. And not only that, but we also rejoice in our afflictions, because we know that affliction produces endurance, endurance produces proven character, and proven character produces hope. This hope will not disappoint us, because God's love has been poured out in our hearts through the Holy Spirit who was given to us.

The Power of Prayer:

[Jas 5:13-15 NLT] Are any of you suffering hardships? You should pray. Are any of you happy? You should sing praises. Are any of you sick? You should call for the elders of the church to come and pray over you, anointing you with oil in the name of the Lord. Such a prayer offered in faith will heal the sick, and the Lord will make you well. And if you have committed any sins, you will be forgiven.

John Spiker,

[1Th 5:23 NLT] Now may the God of peace make you holy in every way, and may your whole spirit and soul and body be kept blameless until our Lord Jesus Christ comes again.

[Act 4:30 NLT] Stretch out your hand with healing power; may miraculous signs and wonders be done through the name of your holy servant Jesus."

[Psa 69:32-33 NLT] The humble will see their God at work and be glad. Let all who seek God's help be encouraged. 33 For the LORD hears the cries of the needy; he does not despise his imprisoned people.

[Mat 11:28-30 NLT] Then Jesus said, "Come to me, all of you who are weary and carry heavy burdens, and I will give you rest. Take my yoke upon you. Let me teach you, because I am humble and gentle at heart, and you will find rest for your souls. For my yoke is easy to bear, and the burden I give you is light."

It is written In Scripture:

[Psa 102:1-2 NLT] 1 A prayer of one overwhelmed with trouble, pouring out problems before the LORD. LORD, hear my prayer! Listen to my plea! 2 Don't turn away from me in my time of distress. Bend down to listen and answer me quickly when I call to you.

[1Pe 3:12 KJV] For the eyes of the Lord [are] over the righteous, and his ears [are open] unto their prayers:

[1Jo 5:15 NIV] And if we know that he hears us--whatever we ask--we know that we have what we asked of him.

[Psa 66:19-20 NLT] But God did listen! He paid attention to my prayer. 20 Praise God, who did not ignore my prayer or withdraw his unfailing love from me.

[Mat 11:28 NLT] 28 Then Jesus said, "Come to me, all of you who are weary and carry heavy burdens, and I will give you rest.

[Phl 4:6 HNV] 6 In nothing be anxious, but in everything, by prayer and petition with thanksgiving, let your requests be made known to God

Psalm 143:11- for the glory of your name, O Lord preserve my life. Because of your faithfulness, bring me out of this distress.

[Jas 5:16 NIV] Therefore confess your sins to each other and pray for each other so that you may be healed. The prayer of a righteous person is powerful and effective.

[1Th 5:23 NLT] Now may the God of peace make you holy in every way and may your whole spirit and soul and body be kept blameless until our Lord Jesus Christ comes again.

[Jer 17:14 NLT] O LORD, if you heal me, I will be truly healed; if you save me, I will be truly saved. My praises are for you alone!

[1Ki 8:28, 30 NLT] Nevertheless, listen to my prayer and my plea, O LORD my God. Hear the cry and the prayer that your servant is making to you today. ... May you hear the

humble and earnest requests from me and your people Israel when we pray toward this place. Yes, hear us from heaven where you live, and when you hear, forgive.

[Mat 6:9-10 KJV] After this manner therefore pray ye: Our Father which art in heaven, Hallowed be thy name. Thy kingdom come. Thy will be done in earth, as [it is] in heaven.

[2Th 3:16 NLT] Now may the Lord of peace himself give you his peace at all times and in every situation. The Lord be with you all.

Players of reflections:

[Psa 35:27 NLT] But give great joy to those who came to my defense. Let them continually say, "Great is the LORD, who delights in blessing his servant with peace!"

[Isa 55:12 NLT] You will live in joy and peace. The mountains and hills will burst into song, and the trees of the field will clap their hands!

[Rom 14:17 NLT] For the Kingdom of God is not a matter of what we eat or drink, but of living a life of goodness and peace and joy in the Holy Spirit.

[Rom 15:13 NLT] I pray that God, the source of hope, will fill you completely with joy and peace because you trust in him. Then you will overflow with confident hope through the power of the Holy Spirit.

www.ingramcontent.com/pod-product-compliance
Lightning Source LLC
LaVergne TN
LVHW012103070526
838202LV00056B/5603